MAKE REALITY TV YOUR REALITY

Crush Your Reality Singing Show Audition
and Ignite Your Music Career

BRIANNA RUELAS

ISBN: 978-1-7355158-0-9 (ebook)
ISBN: 978-1-7355158-1-6 (paperback)

Library of Congress Control Number (LCCN): 2020915313

Dallas, Texas, United States

YOUR FREE GIFT

Your Reality Singing Show Audition Checklist

SHOW UP PREPARED AND READY TO ROCK YOUR AUDITION!

- *Get confident in understanding your true, authentic motivation behind your audition*

- *Learn how to craft your story and your core brand message*

- *Know the 6 most impactful actions you can take to have a successful audition*

https://bit.ly/realitytvchecklist

*I dedicate this book to my mother and biggest fan,
Kay Bailey. Thank you for always believing in me.*

*To my husband and precious daughters,
I will forever be grateful for the selfless way you
support my creative career. May we never
stop growing and dreaming.*

*To my clients, many who've shaped the content of this
book, thank you for trusting me to be a part of your music
journey. You always have someone in your court.*

TABLE OF CONTENTS

SECTION FOUR:
TIME TO SHINE

SECTION FIVE:
IT'S ALL ABOUT THE SPRINGBOARD, BABY

INTRODUCTION

Picture this.

You're on a soundstage, spot lights and cameras transporting you before millions of eyes and ears. You are seen. The world is listening as your voice delivers your message. Millions catch goosebumps through your impactful performance and now they want more.

Wouldn't it be amazing to share your story and talent with millions on a reality singing show? If you're reading this book, this might be your dream.

But **how** can you make this a reality and **where** do you even begin?

Chances are, you fall into one of two categories: The Musician or The Novice.

As the Musician, you're an unsigned independent artist, who's been gigging for years, releasing music and looking for an opportunity to grow your audience and take it to the next level. You've felt a taste of success and you feel like you've tried it all. You desire to separate yourself from the noise, but if you're being honest with yourself, you know you don't need a couple of judges to decide your worth as an artist. Perhaps you've auditioned what feels like an infinite number of times, with no luck and you're ready to explore a new path to success.

As the Novice, you're as green as they come. A bright eyed, newcomer to the music industry, eager to take the world by storm. Perhaps you grew up watching reality singing shows, love to sing and perform and know in your bones, you're meant for this! Problem is, you have no idea where to start, you don't even have a social media following, and you question whether you have what it takes to actually make it.

Welcome, you made it! Congratulations. You've taken the first step to positioning yourself for a successful reality singing show experience.

I recommend getting to know each other while you're here, because this ride they call a Reality Singing Show, is full of artists just like you, at different ages and stages of the game and there is something you can all learn from each other. Believe it or not, you all have something in common. You all desire to make an impact with your music and create a life doing what you love. This book will offer the preparation you need to get there!

INTRODUCTION

Inside *Make Reality TV Your Reality*, I will take you to the beginning and show you the best place to start. I will guide you through creating a clear plan for reality music success and defining your unique artist brand, so you can get noticed and stand out. I will also help you develop a powerful pre-audition strategy that will lead to designing your "chair turning" game plan, so you can showcase your best on audition day. Lastly, I will shine a light on the best way to leverage your reality singing show experience as a launchpad for your music career, so you can use their platform to blow up yours!

This book is interactive and will give you exclusive access through QR code technology to view video trainings and resources, in addition to insight from past reality show contestants and music industry experts, providing their top tips for a successful reality singing show experience.

I've worked with and mentored countless independent artists, to help them establish clear plans and online business strategies for their music career success and coached up many of these same artists to have successful reality show experiences. Through our work and strategic planning together, my clients have raised thousands of dollars in crowdfunding campaigns, released Top Ten iTunes charting new music and grown authentic, true relationships with their fans who are excited to support their music careers.

As a singer/songwriter, I also know how it feels to experience the highs and lows of the creative artist journey. One day you're on top of the world, the next you question whether you really have what it takes to be relevant and relatable with your music. This is what I went through back in Season 4 of *American Idol*.

I got to experience the bitter taste of rejection three times before getting an opportunity to be a part of Season 4 of *American Idol*. Every time I got the, "no thank you, try again next time" line, felt like a punch in the gut. But, it formed grit and resilience—and made my golden ticket offer that much sweeter. Out of 100,000 "hopefuls" that lined up cattle call style that season—, I was 1 of 100.

Unfortunately, things didn't go so well in the audition stage in Hollywood, so when my time on American Idol ended, I was a disaster. The sting of rejection had me bonafide depressed. I spent my days either sleeping or crying and my biggest fear was confirmed. I had given power to the *"lie"* that if you don't make it in the entertainment industry by your early 20's, you're washed up.

What would my family think? What would my friends and teachers back home think? Everyone believed in me, except myself. I had blown my opportunity and now I was officially "washed up."

Thankfully, I woke up to realize this was NOT the end of my story and I don't want it to be yours either. I created this book to flip that ugly "*lie*" upside down.

Make Reality TV Your Reality will not only prepare you on how to position yourself in the best way possible to get noticed and get cast, but it will give you a blueprint to maximize your reality show opportunity and use it as a springboard for future music career growth.

Jo James, a client and Neo-Soul musician from Austin, says, "I honestly don't think I would've made it to the Blinds round on The Voice, without everything Brianna and I did to prepare leading up to L.A."

Jessica Manalo, another client and Indie Soul artist from Las Vegas says, "Working with Brianna and taking her online course, *Make Reality TV Your Reality*, gave me the direction I needed to deliver a confident audition. I got so many ideas I would've never picked up myself. Brianna's got the experience, tips, and tricks to make any singer-songwriter go above and beyond their own expectations!"

The good news is, I promise you don't have to work with me personally to master these tricks and experience success, because I'm delivering them all inside *Make Reality TV Your Reality*. When you commit to doing the work, taking action and recognizing that perhaps you don't have it all figured out, this book will propel to personal and music career growth. I also promise that this book will be the difference in how you approach and slay your audition and ignite massive momentum towards making the music impact you desire.

Don't be the Musician or the Novice that misses out on opportunities to get your music and message heard, allowing fear of rejection or self doubt to get in the way of reaching new heights. Don't wait another day, hoping to be discovered or praying for an opportunity.

Be the kind of artist that others admire and chase after! Let them be amazed and say, "Wow! They didn't waste time. They just went for it and they're doing it!" Be a decision maker and an action taker and do it immediately.

The strategies you're about to read, have been proven to position artists for successful reality singing show experiences and sustainable music career growth. All you have to do is keep reading to find out how. Each chapter will reveal new ways to grow and gain momentum as a performing artist, and will also include insight from past reality show contestants, as well as music industry professionals.

Take control of your life now; make the choice today to take action, and do something big to supercharge your music career.

Section One

YOU GOTTA START SOMEWHERE

CREATE A CLEAR PLAN FOR YOUR REALITY SINGING SHOW SUCCESS

Oh, hello!

I know how excited you must be to dive right in, but I promise you don't want to miss this welcome video below. It's your firestarter to kick off this book adventure in a unique and powerful way! Just pull out your smartphone and scan using your camera or favorite app. Don't have a phone? No problem, you can access the video by visiting this link:
https://scnv.io/book-welcome

Chapter One

YOUR TICKET TO SUCCESS

Take yourself back to the defining moment in which your music dreams were born. What did you imagine your music life would look like? What feelings enter your body when you take yourself back to this time? I'm guessing the images you see are beautiful; filled with the bright lights, energy and excitement!

If you've lost sight of that fire for your music dreams, it's time to bring it back into focus. Choosing to fully live out your dreams includes the roller coaster of emotions that may catch you by surprise. It's possible you didn't expect it to be so difficult or require so much work. Following your dreams is supposed to be fun, right?

Of course it is!

You've probably grown up hearing, "hard work pays off," but when the rubber hits the road, I'm guessing you don't wake up daily, thinking to yourself, "Man! I'm in the mood to do some hard work!" It's a whole lot easier, tending to the fun stuff: The creating! The performing!

Sure, it's "hard work," prepping for a big show, performance, or audition. Or learning a new instrument, or honing your craft. All difficult and requiring skill, but, I'm actually not talking about any of the above. I'm talking soul work here.

"Wait Brianna. I thought this was a book on HOW to get on a reality singing show?" Well, hold your horses, my friend. I got you.

If you want to truly have success on a reality singing show and create sustainable momentum in your music career, you must first have a plan and to create a plan, you must slow down long enough to clearly visualize your destination.

When you ask yourself questions like, "Where am I headed?" What do I truly want my life to look like and **Why** is this important to me, you begin to connect the synapses in your brain to create real change.

Millions have auditioned for reality singing shows over the past 20 years. Thousands have experienced singing in front of millions. Few have actually leveraged and maximized the opportunity as a springboard for their music careers.

Why do you think this is?

Most artists and individuals who make it on reality singing shows, enter the experience unprepared, wide eyed and without a plan.

I'm not suggesting you approach these types of experiences jaded or lacking of awe and wonder, but your music mindset needs to be at the top IF you want to maximize your opportunity.

This chapter marks the beginning of your journey to realizing a crazy awesome experience on a reality singing show. If you apply the strategies you're about to learn, it will also act as a catalyst for a sustainable career in music—so you can do music on your terms—for the rest of your life!

So let's dive in!

When you take the time to ask yourself the hard, difficult, deep dive questions, you step into a chapter of self-transformation, self-awareness, and growth. You also set yourself up to be unstoppable, not only inside this audition process, but in life.

The self care component is very important if you're going to be strong mentally and emotionally, two necessities to survive this reality audition process.

In this chapter, you will explore the importance of having a clear WHY and start by asking yourself, "Why do I want to audition for this show in the first place?"

When I was in my early twenties auditioning for American Idol, my WHY was simple. I loved to sing, and I wanted to find a way to keep music in my life forever. Growing up, the clear path to a music career was through the gatekeepers: Managers, Record Labels and Radio.

I had no clue how to break into the music industry. It felt like a pipe dream and that a dime a dozen "made it." There were no Artist Development programs, no abundance of music schools and certainly not the same level of DIY Music Industry support that we have today. The Music Industry felt like an elite club that only Los Angeles, New York, and Nashville had access to.

Thank goodness for the internet and the DIY Revolution that changed it all. Thanks to social media, we can create true, authentic fans across the world, who will support our careers, cheer us on and be thrilled to be a part of the journey!

And yes! The road hasn't been perfect, and the industry and labels have been flipped upside down, but this evolution has opened doors for common folks like you and me to get that much closer to our dreams.

Reality TV singing shows are a great "foot in the door" to the connections and opportunities that can positively impact your music career. Just like any opportunity, once you get your foot in the door, it's up to you, to keep it there!

So why do you want to be on a reality singing show?

Are you looking for a platform to share your message to millions of people, so you can make an impact in people's lives?

Do you want an opportunity to build your social media following and get that exposure?

Is your WHY faith driven? Perhaps you believe you've been called to go on this reality singing show.

Or maybe your WHY stems from your desire for a life of adventure and a reality singing show would be a fun experience!

Could your WHY be for the networking and connections that could lead to career growth?

Consider these questions right now.

A word of caution. If your WHY is rooted in your desire to get famous and make loads of money, there is a high probability for disappointment and let down. Reality shows are not your antidote to fame and riches.

Your WHY must be emotional and compelling, driving you to reach your goal at all costs, because if you don't, the status quo will leave you miserable.

Your WHY becomes your ticket to success, because it will keep you motivated and going strong, against rejection and when the going gets tough. When you don't make it the first time and you're at your second audition and then your third, your WHY will be the motivator to not give up.

When you believe in yourself and your thoughts and actions line up, you're unstoppable. Having self-belief, along with consistent action towards your goals, is what makes all of the difference.

Whether you're already established in your music career or just starting out, every artist will have a different WHY, but the important thing is that you have one!

Imagine yourself on the show right now. You believe your WHY is super deep, personal and important, but the person next to you is just there to "have fun." Does this make their WHY super shallow? Not necessarily.

Later in the book, I'll dive into the gravity of avoiding comparison, but please lock this in your brain now. Do not waste your time, energy and head space, comparing yourself to other contestants in the audition room or on the show. You're all different and bring something unique to the table.

This is a time where it's acceptable to be selfish. Focus on yourself, focus on the heart, and live out your WHY!

Still unsure of how to figure it out? Below I've created a list of questions that will get you started. Take some time now, grab a fresh journal and explore these. I urge you to NOT skip this exercise. You may think you know the answers, but in most cases, what you desired six months ago or even a year ago, may have changed. It's important to reevaluate your desires, so that you can shift trajectory when needed and ensure you're on the right path to success.

In the next chapter, we'll take it one step further and narrow in your focus, so you can start making big moves towards your goals and dreams.

TAKE ACTION:

1. Why Do You Really Want To Be On This Show In The First Place? List as many reasons as come to mind.

2. Why should your music be shared? What impact do you want to make through your music?

3. What about your current life situation needs to change and what will be the consequence if you do nothing about it?

Chapter Two

YOU GET WHAT YOU FOCUS ON

Your success on a reality singing show, starts with your audition and the mental and physical preparation leading up to it. Inside this chapter, you'll be empowered by your ability to create success in your life, simply by choosing what you focus on.

"True success is creating consistent pleasure in life that causes you to grow and failure is being able to find pain no matter how good it is."

—Tony Robbins, #1 Life & Business Strategist, Entrepreneur, Personal Power

So, what in your life right now fills you with pride or makes you feel successful? Perhaps it's the original song you just finished or your ability to create strong relationships.

Or like many, you may not feel successful at all. If you fall into the ladder, what will it take for you to truly be satisfied with your success? Are your expectations unreasonable, like "I won't be satisfied until I'm as famous as Lady Gaga and make millions every month?"

Pay attention to the expectations you place on your life. It's possible you could be holding yourself back from experiencing joy because all you're focused on is your "LACK OF _____?"

Consider shifting your attention to all the amazing things you do have in your life. When you focus on giving thanks and managing your expectations, not only of yourself, but of others around you, success can be attained through three steps: Know. Act. Repeat.

First you must **KNOW** what you're after! Having clarity on what you want out of your life is the first step to making it a reality!

Next, you must take **ACTION** to create a better present. Get your butt moving! Stop the insanity, recognize what needs to change, and create a plan to move forward. Take a look at your life five years down the road for some inspiration! Imagine what will happen if you do NOTHING!

Lastly, slow down long enough to take a look at your life, see what's working, discard the trash and press **REPEAT**. Shift, bob and weave and try, try again.

Don't forget to celebrate along the way; however great or small! Find something to be proud of! You're a force to be reckoned with, and if you want others to take notice, you must first believe it!

Now, take a look towards your involvement inside a reality singing show. What will it take for you to feel successful here?

A terrific audition? Progressing to the judges round? Making it to the Top 100? Top 20? Top 10?

Winning the show?

"Being on a reality show doesn't legitimize your career or you as a musician. Working hard at your craft does."

—Adam Pickrell, Producer, Music Director, Musician

When I auditioned for American Idol, Season 4, it took me years to acknowledge that I had any form of success from that experience.

In fact, in mind, I was a flat out failure. I made it to the Hollywood rounds and then I blew my shot! In a huge way, which looking back could've been avoided.

Flashback to one of my biggest regrets of that reality show experience:

I had been preparing for months, had an exercise routine in place, and was working with renowned Los Angeles vocal coach, Steven Memel. I felt strong mentally and physically, and my confidence was sky high. On the day I got my golden ticket from Randy, Paula, and Simon, one of the things Randy kept saying was that he loved the rasp in my voice and that it was "very Melissa Etheridge." My song choice was a bit inconsistent, so they wanted to see more of that soulful, rock vibe from me. Naturally, I took the judges' suggestions to heart and began preparing my best Etheridge material.

In the two-month span between receiving my golden ticket and the Hollywood round, I moved apartments. Forgetting to notify *American Idol* of my move was my first mistake in a string of unfortunate events leading to the most horrible audition of my career.

YOU GET WHAT YOU FOCUS ON

[Insert dramatic *"Dun dun dunnn."*]

A week prior to the Hollywood round, I noticed I hadn't received any information on the audition. I called the offices immediately to check in and discovered they had mailed my packet to my old address. Yowza!

I rushed to the *American Idol* offices in Hollywood that afternoon to grab my packet. (Fortunately, I lived in LA at the time and was able to do that.) To my shock and dismay, there was a CD inside the packet with strict instructions to choose two songs from the ten provided. Out of the ten songs, the closest thing to "rock" was "The Letter" by The Box Tops. I chose one more— "Ain't No Mountain High Enough" by Marvin Gaye and Tammi Terrell. All of the time and money I'd invested working my Etheridge material (with LA's top vocal coach Steven Memel) was completely in vain. Well, not completely, because I learned a ton!

Distraught, I set out to learn, polish, and connect to the new material in one week's time. Neither song I chose felt "right" for me, but out of the ten these were my best options.

I didn't have the cash to schedule another vocal lesson with Steven, so I tried to prepare on my own.

This was mistake number two.

For such an important opportunity, I should have found a way to work in one more vocal lesson. In addition to polishing the material, Steven could've also provided valuable input on song choice, as this was not my strong suit.

The day arrived and I made the two-hour drive, fifteen miles over the hill to Hollywood. I recall meeting Adam Lambert briefly and thinking, *Now HE looks like a rock guy!* There was also another Brianna auditioning who had blue hair. The game was on, as I started comparing myself to the other rockers. *Idol* was casting a show, after all, and they needed to fit all their different characters into their neat, perfect squares. As much as I wanted to fit in one of their squares, I knew deep down I was a "divergent": a music mush-pot full of soul, rock, jazz, and Texas.

In our run-through with the music director and accompanist, she informed us of a change in the arrangement for "Ain't No Mountain"; the music break between verses was removed. As we listened to the changes, I struggled with focus and was knocked off my game, leading to fatal mistake number three.

What came next was mortifying.

It was finally my turn to shine, and I entered the stage with confidence. My first song was "The Letter," which should have been sung a few steps higher, so it lacked energy and fell flat. I had one more chance to "wow" the judges with "Ain't No Mountain," but to say I missed the mark is an understatement. This song came across as the *antithesis* of "wow"!

I completely forgot the revised arrangement, and when the second verse started, I paused for the nonexistent music break. The piano continued while the hundred other contestants stared at me from the audience seats. Randy, Paula, and Simon looked confused, going back and forth between the piano and my hot mess. I'll never forget Simon's disappointed face, which communicated, "This is pure rubbish!"

The judges were justified in their disappointment. I was a complete waste of their time that day. "Rubbish" is a great word for how bad I blew my audition, and I am very aware of the mistakes I made. Singing "The Letter" felt forced, and I missed an opportunity to truly make it my own and memorable. In addition to missing the changes in arrangement, "Ain't No Mountain High Enough" was not the best song choice for me either.

The beauty in looking back on this disappointing memory is the wealth of knowledge I gained from it. As they say, hindsight is 20/20. I learned humility, resilience, grit, and perseverance. I can look back now and actually laugh over how terrible I performed that day.

My past does not define me, and quite honestly, when I focus on the success of being chosen as a Top 100 finalist out of the 100,000 that auditioned that season, I feel like a million bucks!

Can we do the math for a moment? I was part of the 0.001%.

Not 1.0%, but 0.001% and that is something to celebrate!

So, allow this chapter to help you reframe your perceptions and view on success! Take action now and grab your journal to answer the questions below. Be honest with yourself and develop your ability to create change.

The next chapter will get you started on Step One To Success, knowing where you're headed! So buckle up for the soul work ahead.

TAKE ACTION:

1.   What is your current definition of success?

2. What are three things you are proud of in your life right now?

3. What will it take for you to feel successful on this reality singing show?

Chapter 3

GET YOUR PLAN ON

Now that you've taken the time to shift your focus and redefine "success," let's start taking action to create it. For starters, please give yourself some grace as you're moving through this book. Remember, you're learning new ways to approach your life and music career and with new ideas, comes discomfort.

Embrace the discomfort. You're headed to growth and growth often takes time.

Inside this chapter, I will uncover the exact steps I take when I'm stuck and need clarity. I'll start by re-introducing my personal inventory process, found inside my first book, *Performing Artist Pathway* and move on to guide you through creating your own personal clarity brain dump. Both go hand in hand in establishing a strong foundation for your personal success and defining your priorities and goals.

Taking personal inventory is the act of slowing down long enough to thoughtfully and intentionally decide what it is that you want. When you conduct your personal inventory, focus on getting real and not answering questions in a way that will be pleasing to others. This inventory is for you, so be honest with yourself and authentic when recording your desires.

"Life moves pretty fast. If you don't stop and look around once in a while, you could miss it."

Ferris Bueller's Day Off

Personal Inventory is also the kind of soul work that's not always fun. It requires thorough answers and thought, which has the potential to bring up pain or uncover insecurities. Throw self judgement to the side and don't hold back.

Look at your current situation and record where you're at today and establish your starting point. Account for your current situation inside your music business. Are you green or at the early stages of your career? Are you questioning whether the music industry is for you?

Perhaps you're at a stage where honing your craft is a priority.

You'll also want to account for your personal life. What's your living situation like? How do you make money? How are your relationships? What do you value most or is there a personal message you want to convey?

Think about areas where you feel you're thriving and others where you're drowning. What is currently working for you? What areas of your life do you feel like you can't even catch a breath?

If you need more framework, please grab your copy of *Performing Artist Pathway* today and carve out time for the soul work necessary to get your heart and mind straight.

GAIN CLARITY ON YOUR NEXT STEPS

Once you've taken the time to thoughtfully work through the personal inventory questions, you can move on to my very favorite exercise to drive focus and creativity with The Clarity Brain Dump.

Brain dumps help you clear out the cobwebs in your mind and shut out the noise long enough to discern what action is needed. I use these brain dumps anytime I'm stuck or in need of re-establishing my priorities. I also use this technique for every creative project I start, including every book and online course I've ever created.

Ultimately, when you don't have a clear path to where you're going, you lack confidence and insecurity settles in. Insecurity breeds paralysis, which halts progress.

"Prior to auditioning for AGT, I really didn't know what I wanted out of my own career and my own understanding of success and fame was non-existent. Have a plan for yourself and an understanding of what your goals are for your experiences and do not let this reality show be the thing that defines it. Let it be a stair step to where you're headed.

There's a big difference between success and fame. Reality tv shows can be a great way to start your career off, as well as, a great way to learn and get your brand out there, but it's not a defining moment."

—Cas Haley, Texas Singer-Songwriter-Guitarist, America's Got Talent Season 2 Runner Up

Understanding what you want is equally important to understanding what you don't want. The Clarity Brain Dump will get you there. It will enable you to move past any boulder getting in your way, so you can start making progress again and have that breakthrough!

Priorities shift as you evolve, so repeating this exercise every three to six months is a smart, productive way to evaluate whether your actions are aligned with your desires.

The illustration below gives you some framework, so feel free to create quadrants on a sheet of paper like the image below, or simply free flow without constriction.

Either way, take all the thoughts cluttering your mind and commit them to paper. Give yourself permission, without judgement to write down every thought you're consumed with in the categories of Personal/Self Care, Home/Relationships, Music Business and Creative Projects.

PERSONAL/ SELF CARE	**HOME/ RELATIONSHIPS**
MUSIC BIZ	**CREATIVE**

You might be thinking, "What does my personal stuff or self care have anything to do with my business?" The answer is EVERYTHING.

I'm a believer that your personal and business life are interconnected and if your mindset and belief systems are a disaster, it will impact your career success. It will also severely get in the way of you having a powerful audition. When you take a holistic approach to your life and address all the areas that contribute to your success and well being, you'll thrive in ways you've never imagined.

As you're working through your brain dump, consider everything you want to see happen in your music business and career. Are there areas that need improvement or do you have old, worn out belief patterns that need replacing? Do you need to level up your knowledge, take an online course or even hire a coach?

When addressing the creative section, think of projects that will get you fired up. Say yes to the ones that make you feel amazing and energized. Say "heck no" to creative projects that feel like a drag. Your energy is precious. Your energy is time. Time is Money. Use it wisely.

When you say no to things that don't excite you, you free yourself up to receive opportunities that align more with your gifts and desires. You also step into an empowered state through your choice to follow through on your priorities.

Give yourself ten minutes tops to rapidly put pen to paper. Use all the colors of the rainbow if it suits your fancy. Once you finish, look at your page and start identifying any connections, repetitive thoughts or commonalities on the page.

From there, circle three items that really stand out as your biggest priorities to date. These are the priorities that if you focus on them intently over the next 90 days, you can realistically accomplish them. Write them down and rank them from one to three.

Your top priority is one that will move the needle most in your career and life—if you dedicate your time and focus on this one thing. Think and write down that number one thing in your life that you'd like to accomplish. This will open doors in other areas for you to move forward with grace and ease.

Your first priority may be to get informed when reality singing shows are casting. Ensure these auditions are on your radar and sign up to receive alerts by visiting the individual show sites. Below are audition information links to three of the top American talent competition shows, so you can explore how to get more information or apply for your next audition today!

America's Got Talent:
https://www.americasgottalentauditions.com/

The Voice:
https://www.nbcthevoice.com/

American Idol
https://abc.com/shows/american-idol/auditions

Congratulations! You're ready to define your top three priorities you must take action on! It's important to take them one at a time. Focused action is what gets the job done. Do not spread yourself too thin or become distracted. Zero in on the target and don't let anything get in the way of you reaching the finish line.

Scared to take action? Just consider how you will feel three months from now when you attack these priorities and get them done. Let that glorious vibe settle in.

Feels good doesn't it?

Now, how would you feel if you ignored them? Allow your positive projections to fuel your fire.

This chapter has ignited you towards action and put into perspective your priorities. You may be feeling overwhelmed or even a desire to change your day to day approach to life. Just remember, this is a process and journey. Change doesn't happen overnight, so give yourself grace and know that this takes time. Focus on taking consistent action right now by carving out your plan below and keep moving forward.

In the next chapter, you'll clearly define your unique artist brand, so you can get noticed by casting producers and stand out!

TAKE ACTION:

1. Write Down Your Number One Priority or Goal.

2. Record the action steps you must take to reach this goal.

3. Remove all distractions and stay laser focused on the prize. Address one distraction below and how you can keep on course.

4. Write down one thing you will do to celebrate when you accomplish your goal.

Section Two

ARE YOU CLEAR OR CONFUSING?

BUILD A ROADMAP TO DEFINE YOUR UNIQUE ARTIST BRAND

Chapter 4

BE THE COMPLETE PACKAGE

One of the most consistent pieces of advice I hear from past reality singing show contestants, is this: "Know who you are as an artist." If you don't know WHO you are as an artist, how will the casting director or producer know?

Inside this chapter, you'll define your artist vibe, and how to communicate a very clear description of who you are as an artist and what you want to bring to the table. In order for you to be the complete package casting directors and producers are looking for, you need to have all the puzzle pieces tied together.

YOUR ARTIST VIBE

It's paramount to have a hyper clear artist vibe, because a confused producer or casting director, will not cast you. Your Artist Vibe is an alignment of your sound, song choice, look and personality and helps producers and casting directors know where you fit inside their show.

Ultimately, your vibe is your brand and this is all part of Marketing 101. The word "Marketing" might scare you, but isn't one of your top goals as a performing artist to share your message? Marketing is essential to make your music impact and is a large part of MAXIMIZING this entire reality singing show experience.

When you consistently convey who you are as an artist and get comfortable sharing your brand, the spread of your music impact begins and others will take notice.

As a reminder, this reality singing show is about more than just your voice. It's entertainment television and your talent, story, look, personality and energy all work towards your marketability on their show.

Because of this, it is critical you come to the table in an authentic way that helps people understand and relate to who you are. Reality singing shows are tricky because you have to blend your true personality with your artist persona. You must connect them in a seamless way and for many this is a challenge.

When I auditioned for American idol, I was fresh off the musical theatre boat. I had no clue who I was an artist, I just knew I wanted to sing.

BE THE COMPLETE PACKAGE

As I entered the audition room, I carried myself similar to walking onto a stage to audition for *West Side Story* or *A Chorus Line*. My tone of voice in my introduction was very polished and proper. It did not reflect my personality in any fashion, nor was it how I'd speak in a real conversation with a friend. It did not make sense for this reality show.

Hindsight is 20/20. After years of watching reality singing shows and coaching my clients to be on them, I now know better. Sure, I made it to Hollywood, but looking back, I realize my success on the show could've looked differently had I relaxed a bit and let them see my true personality.

Allowing others to experience your personality is very important. All of the development work you did in the first section comes to play in your audition. Clarity and focus, translates into confidence and security. This state of mind enables you to put your best foot forward inside the audition and clearly communicate the positive energy you'll bring to the show.

Take the collective personal inventory data you've identified and determine how it parlays into you as an artist. Bring your true, authentic self, which is what people are going to resonate with, and let it shine through your songwriting, performance and artistry overall. You have a solid ground to stand on because you're confident in your convictions, understand your values and the message you want to share.

At your core, this **IS** who you are as an artist.

"Be confidently and genuinely yourself throughout the entire process. Do not decide you would have a better chance, in a different genre, dressed liked someone else, because ultimately, all you'd be doing is putting on a costume and doing something unfamiliar. Your competition will be people who have lived and breathed the genre for years. Be 100% yourself because if you don't make it, at least you have a great learning experience and have made some great contacts. If you do make it, you'll have a better chance of going further inside the show, because you will be genuine."

—Katrina Cain, Melancholy Pop Artist, The Voice Season 15

YOUR ARTIST SOUND

The next step to nailing your Artist Vibe is to address your Artist Sound. When people ask what type of artist you are, know the genre you most identify with and have the ability to clearly communicate your sound.

Would you describe your music as rhythm heavy or rich in melodies? Practice effective communication and use descriptors that enable producers and casting directors to get a clear glimpse into the type of music you create. This will provide them something to identify with.

Put yourself in the shoes of the listener. How are they going to feel when they hear you sing or listen to your music? Who will they compare you to? How would **they** describe your music?

One creative way to get feedback is to take a poll and conduct a little investigation. Ask your existing fans or those you love around you to take a listen to your music and describe what they hear or what the first thing that comes to mind is when they listen to your music. Often, outside perspective is the quickest way to gather information and discover new insight about ourselves.

But be ready; the feedback you'll receive may surprise you. Either way, the importance is in the understanding of how others relate to you and your music when they hear it. This is valuable information that will help you connect authentically moving forward.

When you get a clear understanding of your sound, try to identify the nuances that make your voice unique and set you apart. This will enable you to niche down wherever possible.

For example, if you're a country girl from Tennessee, maybe you identify with country-rock. You're still country, but a little edgier. This is different from mainstream country, correct?

There are different levels and niches inside every genre, but the important thing is to embrace your sound and be consistent. No one wants to be stifled or put inside a box when it comes to their artistry, but remember you are being cast for a reality singing show that is looking for diversity.

They don't need 14 country singers inside one season, so you must fall into a specific genre or category that works for their show and there cannot be any confusion.

For casting, make it evidently known where you belong in their season lineup. They only have room for a few artists in each category: Country, Pop, Pop-Rock, Atl-Pop, R&B, Soul, Rock, etc. Keep in mind that if you come to the audition and your artist vibe is confusing, it will be extremely difficult for them to cast you.

YOUR ARTIST LOOK

Another part of establishing your Artist Vibe comes down to your look. For example, what colors do you resonate with and does your wardrobe reflect that? Are you a hat person? What's going to help you express your unique character and stand out?

If you're not a hat person, please don't wear a hat thinking it will get you attention. An authentic Artist Vibe requires an authentic, steady Artist Look. You want to make an impression from the moment you enter the audition door, so that show producers and casting directors see someone they can work with. Your signature look is what also makes you memorable!

Most importantly, be consistent and have the awareness that when people see you on television, they are going to instantly have an opinion of whether they relate to you or not, based on what you look like. Whatever look or brand colors you choose to embody, commit fully and stick with it.

"Creating your artist character is an exaggeration of who you are as a performer, separate from who you are as a person. Your artist persona is an amplified version of who you are currently, and gives the world something to latch onto. It's really important for your fans and the public to have somebody to identify with; someone they feel connected with. Having a consistent look feels familiar and sets an expectation for us as fans. So think about your staple pieces and feature accessories that you will always wear. Maybe it's a set of rings—and those might change—but they're always chunky and part of your image. If you're the rocker guy, just bump it up a notch: use scarves, wear bracelets and necklaces. Try the eyeliner look. Do some research and see if you can pull things from past rockstars to incorporate into your artist character."

—Meagan D'Von Funk, Creative Consultant & Director of Loft Stories

Inside your audition, you'll get 15 to 30 seconds to shine and create an unforgettable performance. You have a very short amount of time to make an impression and allow casting to see the type of artist you are. From your introduction, artist look and song choice to your personal conviction, you must tie these components together and translate confidently, or your 15 seconds will come and go very quickly.

Unfortunately, if you neglect the importance of nailing your Artist Vibe, you could be left disappointed because you did not prepare. Do not underestimate the power of the full package: your look, your song choice, your talent and personality must align to create your full marketing package.

Remember, if you walk into an audition room looking like a rocker, but when you open your mouth, your sound reflects deep Texas country, confusion will set in because your look and sound do not align. At the end of the day, producers, casting directors, and judges simply have too many artists to review, to spend time and energy on anything complicated.

In this chapter, you created clarity around establishing a solid Artist Vibe. Take some time now to pull out your journal and answer the questions below. In the next chapter, you'll learn how you can get the attention of casting directors through a rock solid social media game plan.

TAKE ACTION:

How can you stand out through your Artist Vibe? Journal all of the nuances that set you apart as a performing artist. From the texture of your voice or music niche to your appearance, what will you do to make a distinct impression and kick your creative brand image up a notch?

Chapter 5

CONSISTENT CONTENT = CONSISTENT BRAND

In order to leverage the reality singing show platform, it's important to create consistent messaging through your social media platforms and present an accurate view of your artist brand. Casting directors and producers will take a look at your social media accounts before, during, and after you get cast. In fact, many artists will be invited for private auditions, solely from the attention their social media platforms are giving them. In this chapter, you'll learn why you must prioritize your social media aesthetics to attract the interest of casting directors.

To establish a strong presence on social media, you can start by identifying who your followers and fans are. To create engagement and eventually make that music impact you're seeking, you must know who you're talking to. When you identify who you're talking to, you can connect more effectively. Ultimately this will also lead to growth in your audience, because you'll also know where to find them.

If you don't have fans quite yet or are just getting started, think about who you want your fans to be? Perhaps there's an artist you admire or one similar to you. What are their fans like and could they possibly become yours?

Utilizing the free analytics tools inside your social media business account will tell you a lot about your followers. Insights, such as visitor activity, help you learn when your followers are most active on social media. Other insights on audience demographics and content will show which posts attracted the most views and help you establish basic demographics for your fans. You'll learn how old they are, where most of your followers live and may even discover you have a global fan base.

All of your online content needs to align with your artist vibe and brand image. Fans and followers desire consistency and they also want someone to relate to. Does your visual content reflect your sound or are you presenting a confusing representation of who you are as an artist?

"People need a reason to invest before they ever click on your profile. When they do visit your website or socials, it is important that you don't look one way then sound another. You don't want to market yourself one way, visually, and have a totally different sound that associates you with another kind of artist. There are too many musicians in the world for your brand to be confusing when people search for a new artist, so make sure what they see is what they will get."

—Meagan D'Von Funk, Creative Consultant & Director of Loft Stories

HAVE A SOCIAL PLAN

Another way to clearly communicate your artist brand is to establish a clear message and plan for what you want to talk about. What do you have to say? At the top of this book, you answered who you are, what you want, and your "Why", so pull from that and write down the things that you value most.

Think of specific causes that spark excitement or viewpoints you want to relate with your fans on. Don't be afraid to tie in your real, personal interests; like how you spend your time. Fans desire to relate to you on a personal level.

One interest I love sharing is my love for road tripping with my family. There's a sense of peace and clarity I get on the road, so anytime I take a trip, those photos don't fully consume my feed, but I do add them to my story to share my insights and connect with my audience.

Share the quirky parts of you that are light and funny. Many of your fans on social media are there, because they want to be entertained. There is enough darkness in the world, so why not be a consistent light they can enjoy?

Above all, have a plan in place to deliver a solid communication strategy. This will help you establish consistency inside your feed and will also keep you from posting randomly, simply because you haven't shared in days.

"People don't connect with content—people connect with people. So if you're sharing posts like, "Gig coming up this Friday, don't miss it!", you're missing out on an opportunity to connect with your audience in a meaningful way. When an artist writes these types of posts in a last-minute rush to fill their feed, I call it "panic-posting." Instead, why not tell a story about a song you're performing, or talk about how you overcame stage fright and now look forward to performing more than anything else? Take the task of advertising your gig as a chance to share something meaningful about you or your music.

The best way to avoid panic-posting is by planning your content, posting with purpose, and offering up more than just simple announcement captions. Start forging connections by being a consistent, strong presence online. Your audience will be more drawn to you and you'll end up with a loyal fanbase."

—Megan Kuhar, Creative Brand Coach

Once you answer the questions of who you are as an artist, your interests and what you value most, you can begin to carve out your social media pillars that act as a framework for your online content. Pillars help to establish consistency inside your feed and will also keep you from posting randomly, simply because you haven't shared in days. Create four to five pillars for yourself and when you plan content or go to post, ask yourself, does this content fall under one of my pillar categories?

An example of my pillars and ideas I post on would look something like:

1. Planning and the importance of knowing your desired outcome

2. Performing artists & encouraging them on their journey

3. Reality TV audition prep & maximizing your experience with online business strategies

4. Travel & cool places to discover

5. Coaching & the importance of getting the support you need

CONSISTENT CONTENT = CONSISTENT BRAND

An example from my client, Jo James:

1. Music: videos, album artwork, lyrics, releases

2. Live & online performances

3. Dogs, Wife, Family

4. Personal Cause: Obesity and Crohn's & Colitis

5. Endorsements, Sponsorships

Another example from my client, Kaatii:

1. Music: guitar, instruments, songwriting

2. Music I Love: other artists and music experiences

3. Playful Personality Posts

4. Cat Lady

5. Live Kaatii performances

As you can see from all three examples above, each set of pillars has one "off brand" pillar. For Jo, it's dogs, for me it's travel and for Kaatii, it's cats. Yours might be your obsession for pizza or extreme adventure. The important thing to remember, is to not allow these "off brand" pillars to consume your social media feed. They do make for great story posts though!

When you "pepper" these quirky posts inside your feed, it creates separation and breadth and also gives your fans and followers deeper insight into your true personality, allowing them to connect with you in a new way.

ARTIST BRAND CULTURE

Now it's your turn! Below, I've included exclusive access inside my online course "Make Reality TV Your Reality," to walk you through the Artist Brand Culture exercise. I use this marketing vehicle inside the online course and with my clients to help them get clear on their messaging and establish a foundation for their social media pillars.

To create your clear message for social media and inside the reality singing show interview process, scan the QR code below or click the link here https://scnv.io/br-culture and get free access to this video training. Coming up in the next chapter, you'll learn how to choose songs that will highlight your strengths and get you the "Yes!"

CONSISTENT CONTENT = CONSISTENT BRAND

Chapter 6

LET YOUR SONG MAKE YOU, NOT BREAK YOU

There are many stages of the reality singing show audition process. The very first stage of the audition process is typically in front of casting directors or line producers. You are responsible for your song choice in these initial auditions and making a strong first impression is immensely critical.

Depending on how far you take your reality singing show journey, you'll have critical song choice decisions every step of the way. Inside this chapter, you'll learn how to choose songs that will highlight your strengths and help you progress to the next round of the audition process.

If and when you successfully "wow" the line producers or casting directors, you will proceed to the second stage of the audition process. Every show is different, but typically this will take place in front of another set of producers. Often these are the Executive Producers of the show, and they are the big decision makers. If you thought the first stage was important, multiply the gravity exponentially, as the Executive show producers ultimately have final say at every stage of the reality competition game.

The final stage of the audition process is the gateway to getting on the show. In most cases this is the stage where you get the opportunity to showcase your performance before celebrity judges. In this round, the music department of the show will contact you with a list of approved songs to sing before the judges and make their final recommendations.

Each stage of the competition holds a different set of requirements and things to prepare, but for now, we are simply going to focus on the first two. Whether you're in charge of choosing your own songs or asked to choose songs from an approved list, song choice strategy will position you to get cast.

SONG CHOICE STRATEGY ONE

The first strategy might seem obvious, but you must ask yourself several questions:

"What song will highlight my unique personality and vocal strengths, and above all, entertain?"

LET YOUR SONG MAKE YOU, NOT BREAK YOU

"What song is going to show that I'm relevant and relatable to audiences and the current popular music landscape?"

In the first stage of the audition process, you must choose a song that delivers a punch and demonstrates everything you've got. In other words, you must clearly show the producers that you belong on this show and you have what it takes to keep bringing the heat!

In the first stage of the competition, one song is not going to cut it. I recommend at least four songs in your "back pocket" that will all impress and move you closer to the final casting point. What's the "back pocket?" This is your reality show song catalogue or inventory, containing 3-5 options that showcase your absolute best.

Many reality singing show producers want you to choose songs that are up-tempo, entertaining and relevant to what people are listening to on the radio today. If ballads are your sweet spot, choose one that kicks them in the gut and for your second song, deliver an equally powerful uptempo song to demonstrate your versatility. Consult with a vocal coaching expert to determine what song style is best for you to lead with.

During the audition process, casting directors and producers sit in rooms for hours at a time. You want to be so entertaining and energetic, that you wake them up, compel them to listen and subsequently give you that green light to move forward. They're casting an entertainment show and if you can compel them to say yes, you can also win over the viewers.

Most importantly, if you zing them with a performance that's exciting and interesting, and deliver high energy, this will make you memorable. Ultimately, that's what they're looking for. They want someone memorable.

SONG CHOICE STRATEGY TWO

The second strategy is to avoid songs that are too big and bring attention to your weaknesses as a vocalist. Be sure to highlight your strengths, and not make the same mistake I did during my American Idol auditions.

Thankfully, I had an extensive "back pocket" during my audition, but I got to my fourth song on several attempts. During my first attempt in Las Vegas, my fourth song was not enough. The producer literally told me, "You're so close. Please come back and try again." This was after delivering four songs and giving everything I had!

I was devastated, but the truth of the matter is, I should've never allowed it to go that far in the first place. My first two songs should've been so powerful, that the producers didn't question whether I had what it took or not. The kicker to drive home my point is that the songs that made up my "back pocket", were primary ballads. Additionally, they were all obscure songs that were not on the radio and hence, irrelevant.

Moral of the story. Choose songs that are upbeat, entertaining and relevant to what people are listening to on the radio today. Also, make sure your songs thread together seamlessly. Don't choose one rock song, one pop song and a country hit. Create flow and allow your "back pocket" to act as one cohesive group.

SONG CHOICE STRATEGY THREE

The last strategy to implement comes into play once you've chosen your songs: Find a way to make them yours! Don't alter the songs so severely that they are unrecognizable, but arrange and deliver them differently or in a unique way that sets you apart. This is one way to align your song choice with your artist vibe.

Another way is to bend genre-lines in order to create a new interpretation of a song. This can help you stay relevant without abandoning your authenticity. As an example, find a way through your unique arrangement and vocal ability, to make a hit pop song translate in the country or rock space you identify with. Or visa versa.

Choosing how you deliver a song in a way that best suits your voice, is contingent on your confidence as an Artist. In my teens and early twenties, artist development was not taught. I had no idea who I was an artist, or what that even meant. I just knew I wanted to sing. That will no longer cut it in today's music industry. There is simply too much access to information and coaching to ignore this area. If you choose to ignore it, it's guaranteed there are thousands of musicians and artists out there who will have a leg up on you—they've done the work and have confidence in who they are and the authenticity they bring.

When I finally made it to the celebrity judges on American Idol, I had still not mastered my song choice. Although I showed them enough to proceed to the next round in Hollywood, I confused them with my song choices.

Randy Jackson told me my song choice didn't suit my voice and that I'd be better off singing "something like a Melissa Etheridge or something rock." Simon Cowell said he liked the "style of the song, but felt it was just boring."

Both of them were absolutely correct. I was all over the map with my song choice and I share this with you to show you and to implore you to be smart and consistent when it comes down to choosing your songs. Your material must run together cohesively and clearly represent you as an artist.

If you're someone who's on the fence about auditioning with an original song, make sure it's a hit! This is very risky because as an original, it's automatically obscure and could potentially come across as unrelatable. The pros of sharing your original material, especially if it's a great song, is that it will demonstrate your musicianship, artistry and provide an opportunity to showcase your original work. Depending on the show, it might even make it to air.

If you have a flicker of doubt, consult an expert to affirm that your original music will stand the test and secure success for you in the audition room. If it's questionable, have the song in your back pocket, versus leading with it as your first impression.

Want my opinion? Get on my calendar and schedule your audition consult today!
(https://bit.ly/auditionprep60)

MUSIC CAREER CONSULTING
& REALITY AUDITION PREP

bit.ly/auditionprep60

It's time to take action! Right now, grab your journal or open a google document and create two columns. In the first column, write down every potential song for your reality tv music catalogue. These are the songs that you can knock out of the park and can perform in your sleep.

In the second column, write a list of songs that interest you and resonate with your Artist Vibe or genre. These could be potential songs that you need to master before the audition. The more relevant the better to build a powerful music repertoire for your "back pocket."

This will also serve you down the road as you progress in this reality tv show process, because when you get cast, you'll be asked to learn a lot of new material. Prepare for that now by listening to different genres, current hits and past hit songs. You might even spin a classic old school hit into something fresh that listeners will want to fall in love with all over again.

You now have a clear understanding that song choice can make or break your audition, so it's critical to choose songs that highlight your strengths and show off your talent. This will help producers and casting directors have a clear direction on who you are as an artist and where you'll fit inside their show. As mentioned before, the chances of a confused producer casting you in their show are slim to none, so consistency, energy and confidence in your artist brand is very important when you're choosing your material.

Get ready to suit up your armor. Up ahead in the next chapter, you'll learn how to become a warrior of discipline, so you can be strong, positive, flexible, and armed with stamina as you slay your reality tv singing show experience.

Section Three

POSITION YOURSELF
FOR AUDITION SUCCESS

DEVELOP A POWERFUL
PRE-AUDITION STRATEGY

Chapter 7

BECOME A WARRIOR

Do you have what it takes to endure months of unknown tangibles, vocal and physical exhaustion, mental fatigue and emotional stress? Were you expecting your reality tv singing show experience to be a walk in the park?

Reality TV singing shows create a unique and pressure filled set of circumstances in order to facilitate tension that leads to entertaining television. The good news is, you can prepare mentally, physically and emotionally in advance in order to combat stress that can negatively impact your performance.

In this chapter, you'll learn how to become a warrior of Discipline and create a strong mindset to get your body healthy, physically, mentally, and spiritually. This will ultimately prepare you for reality TV singing show battle. Sound scary? Only if you're not focused and prepared with your combat arsenal: a rock solid mindset.

This experience will stretch you in ways you never imagined. You will doubt your ability to perform. You will question your level of talent and expertise and you will be submerged in the uncharted waters of scenarios and circumstances you've never been placed in before. Whether this is your first attempt at reality singing show success or you're returning to battle to try again, you must be able to sustain the entire process and make it to the finish line healthy.

There will be times during your audition process when it will be extremely tempting to allow comparison to settle in, so prepare your mind to be completely bombarded by a lot of noise. In every nook or corner of the audition space, there will be someone flexing their singing chops or rehearsing their material. Even the bathrooms are full of contestants taking advantage of the acoustics.

To create a warrior mindset for mental toughness, start with the three D's.

Discipline is the anchor of the 3 D's and holds everything together. It's the action you take to reach your goals. Discipline will take you from thinking about something, to actually doing something about it.

Desire is the Want and the Why and reinforces how hungry you are to succeed.

Determination is the grit that keeps you pressing forward despite rejection and above all odds.

DAILY SUCCESS HABITS

Daily success habits are also key in ensuring you have a warrior mindset for peak performance inside this competition. Daily success habits are things you can do every single morning or every single day that will set you up for success. Designing daily success habits in advance will pay it forward in the future.

Everyone's daily success habits or rituals look differently. For me personally, I'm an early bird, so getting up at the crack of dawn gets my creative mojo flowing. Waking up early is not ideal for everyone, but for me, I am most productive, creative, and supercharged to live my best life when I start my day off strong.

My daily success ritual looks something like this:

4:30am Alarm goes off: "Ugh... Really? Can't I sleep another 10 minutes?"

"Yes, yes you can." So I do.

5a-6:30am: Write, Create, Brainstorm, Plan.

6:30am – 7:30am : Exercise Time. Walk or run outside in nature while listening to empowering music or podcasts. During the school year, this is wake up time for my three girls to get up and at 'em!

7:30am-8am: Journal/Pray/Meditate & Breathe/Practice Giving Thanks

9am: Go time! Let's hit it!

The rest of the day, come what may. I am mentally and spiritually ready for anything and open to giving my best.

Your daily routine may look starkly different from mine above, but steer clear of comparison. Only you know what is best for you to work efficiently, creatively and inspired. Take meditation for example. Although research shows that most successful people meditate daily, this can be a little intimidating at first.

Before I truly embraced the power of slowing down to breathe, I used to think meditation looked like a skinny man, with long, dark hair, closing his eyes and sitting cross legged with his pinkies in the air. Seemed a little woo woo and out there for me, which led me to believe it wasn't for me.

Meditation doesn't have to be a scary thing; afterall, is breathing scary? Deep breathing is proven to boost oxygen levels to your bloodstream and cleanse your body of toxins on a cellular level. The restorative capabilities our bodies have are truly remarkable; when we tap into them.

In my experience, meditation and deep breathing have also offered immense clarity in how I approach my life and business. Taking breaks to include physical exercise are equally powerful. It sources blood flow through the brain, promoting focus and energy; another healthy choice to get your mind strong.

To create your own set of daily success habits, start by analyzing what your current day to day looks like. Are you running around frantically? Are you semi productive, but know you could probably be using your time more wisely? Start designing your life in a way that will create ease and ignite you with energy to live life intentionally.

Cut out habits that are no longer serving you and think on what might support you as you prepare for this reality singing show experience. This might mean transitioning from five daily caffeine breaks to one. Or establishing an exercise ritual that you actually look forward to. Remove negative habits and replace them with ones that will support you for success, so you can stay clear on your objectives for this competition, eliminate distraction, and feel great in the process.

Take this book for instance. You picked it up because you were hopeful it would offer clarity and position you to get cast on a reality singing show. Committing to carving out time in your daily routine to read and finish this book is a positive action you can take to create success for yourself.

So what will it take for you to finish this book? Create a plan now to get to the finish line. Start by time blocking inside your calendar the specific days and hours you will read and implement the exercises inside this book. This will set yourself up for the best opportunity for success. As the saying goes, "if it's not in your calendar, it's not real."

Now is the time to become a disciplined warrior, by creating positive healthy habits that will carry you through this entire competition. Spoiler alert! These new daily success rituals will translate way beyond this reality experience, and create a personal success foundation for your entire life.

How will you create your warrior mindset? Inside this chapter, you got a glimpse of how daily success rituals could transform your life and set you up to be a force inside this reality show experience. Take some time now to pull out your journal and answer the questions below to design your personal daily success habits.

In the next chapter, you will create a plan to condition your voice with the stamina needed to endure the duration of the competition and avoid a competition ending injury.

TAKE ACTION:

1. What do my current daily habits look like?

2. What habits will help me feel most successful inside my day?

3. When will I carve out time to finish this book?

(ie: How Many Days a week? How Many Minutes a Day? Which Days?)

Chapter 8

CONDITION YOUR VOICE TO LAST

Do not underestimate the importance of preparing vocally for this reality TV singing show. It is a SINGING competition, which means you will be SINGING a lot! Your schedule will not be ideal either. There will be late nights and early mornings, stress and pressure. All of these components combined are a perfect recipe for vocal injury when you're not sufficiently trained. In this chapter, you will create a plan to condition your voice with the stamina needed to endure the duration of the competition and avoid a competition ending injury.

GET PROFESSIONAL SUPPORT

Now is the time to strengthen your vocal chops and get the support you need to get vocally fit. Don't fall into the trap of thinking "I got this, everyone says I'm a great singer" and relying on your natural God-given talents to squeeze your way by. The truth is, having a professional opinion and working with a vocal coach will make a huge difference in your rate of success for getting on the show and progressing throughout the rounds.

The top athletes in the world, and even top thought leaders and business professionals all have coaches. If you truly want to realize success on a reality singing show, why wouldn't you take the extra step and hire a professional to train you to reach your highest potential? Getting with a professional often makes that "golden ticket" or "chair turn" difference.

"There will be a lot of things inside this competition that are out of your control, but professional help IS in your control. I don't care if you're the most talented person, when you stand in line for five hours at a time, your mind is going to mess with you. Getting with the professional, is what will enable you to stay focused despite the chaos around you."

—Tiffany VanBoxtel, Vocal Coach and Founder of The Star Singer Green Room

This point made by expert vocal coach and founder of the Star Singer Green Room, Tiffany VanBoxtel is extremely accurate; especially inside the reality tv singing show audition realm. When you have absolute confidence in your ability to execute your performance and turn on that switch when it's go-time, the long lines, distractions and drama ensuing all around you, will not interfere with you delivering a powerful performance.

Vocal coaching professionals can offer constructive advice and help you take a song a new direction, making it your own. As we touched on in Chapter 6, "making it your own" is one way to create a compelling, exciting performance that is unique and memorable. A vocal coach will also foster confidence, not only in the delivery of your song, but in your ability to sustain the duration of the competition.

When you make the choice to level up and work with a vocal professional to establish your vocal routine and strengthen your voice, you won't have to question, "am I ready or am I good enough?" You'll be prepared and secure in your vocal ability, so you can focus on the goal of delivering your absolute best *and* getting cast!

VOCAL EXERCISE ROUTINE

The physical and mental demands are high once you get on a reality singing show, and a vocal exercise routine will prepare you beyond the audition. Vocal stamina and strength will be paramount over the next six months, as the demand on your voice grows. Having a solid plan in place leading up to your audition, will enable you to push your vocal limits without hesitation and without injury.

"Your voice isn't the same every day, so when you take the time to build in these vocal exercises, spending 15 minutes a day practicing, and knowing what's usual, what's regular, what's irregular, you'll learn how to adjust and overcome it. This not only puts your mind in a good place, but it also allows you to assess the situation before you go in. And that's really powerful."

—Tiffany VanBoxtel, Vocal Coach and Founder of The Star Singer Green Room

Don't underestimate the importance of healthy vocal habits leading up to your audition experience. Preparation and consistency also create a greater awareness to resist any vocal overextension that might take place, due to sleep deprivation, allergies or fatigue.

This chapter drove home that this is a competition, and if you want to compete, your singing voice must be in tip-top shape. The only way for you to get it there, is to put in the hard work and effort so you can be at the height of your game. If you show up unprepared—and are not at the top of your game—you'll be sent home with a head full of regrets, because you weren't ready.

Avoid self-sabotage due to a lack of preparation. By not putting the pre-work in, you're severely limiting your potential. Get yourself in a prime position so that when opportunity knocks, you're there and ready to grab it by the horns!

Will you be vocally prepared when your audition day arrives? Do not let this opportunity pass without giving it your absolute all. Hiring a vocal coach and establishing a consistent vocal exercise routine are only one piece of the puzzle. In the next chapter, you'll learn valuable audition success tips and the common mistakes to avoid.

Chapter 9

AUDITION MISTAKES TO AVOID

Although there are many intangibles completely out of your control on reality singing shows, when you prepare yourself and know what to expect, you set yourself up for the best possibility for success. Inside this chapter, you will further prepare for your big audition day and also learn pre-audition success tips to help you avoid three most common mistakes.

MISTAKE ONE

The first mistake many contestants make is highly avoidable. They don't read the Rules and Guidelines created for the audition, and miss what is being asked of them. For example, something as simple as not showing up with the prepared documents, like a valid ID to prove your age. Or auditioning for a show that you're not eligible for because you're either too young or too old.

Each show will have a different set up requirements. Some might prefer the first audition to be solely acapella. Others require and prefer a backing track. Many auditions will allow you to play an instrument or bring someone to accompany you. Inform yourself of the show's requirements, in advance and prepare accordingly.

Key Tip: If you're a musician who's used to accompanying yourself with an instrument and the audition requires you to sing acapella, practice without the instrument in advance. Your instrument has most likely become an extension of your performance, so it's paramount to rehearse without it. If you progress in the show, this will prepare you when producers ask for a performance sans instrument.

Avoid Mistake One by educating yourself or visiting the FAQ's section on each website. Taking ten minutes to ensure you know where to be, what to bring and how to prepare will alleviate you from any unnecessary stress on audition day, so you can focus on performing your best.

MISTAKE TWO

The second common mistake contestants make occurs during the delivery of their audition material. The singer is solely focused on technique or sounding good, versus creating a compelling and engaging performance and showcasing their personality as well. By mastering the art of personal connection, an artist can take a cover and perform it like an original.

"This is a reality show first and a singing competition second. They are looking for specific people to fit the "character descriptions," and I didn't realize this the first time I auditioned. I relied solely on my musical ability, but you're also supposed to have a personality and they're looking for someone who has character. It's not all about talent."

—Tippy Balady, Soulful Pop Artist, American Idol Season 16

How exactly can you do that? Through a little process I take my clients through called the Song Dissection Process and use of The Emotion to Real Life Inventory. Equipping yourself with this knowledge can be the difference maker between a good performance and a memorable one. It will also translate further by giving you an edge once you make the show, and are asked to sing a multitude of songs that are not your own.

We will go more in depth on this in chapter ahead, but as a quick note, reality singing shows have a large catalogue of approved music they've acquired the rights or license to. This gives them permission to use and air the song on live television. If you're an artist who has a ton of original songs under your belt, chances of you sharing them are unfortunately low. In most cases, the producers will recommend pre-approved songs for you to perform, so it's up to you to bring the heat during your live performance.

The Song Dissection process has five simple steps. Work through these steps in order every time you're learning a new song, so you can save time, alleviate stress and create that all important, "give 'em goose bumps" connection to the material.

STEP ONE: LISTEN

Take time to listen to the new song a few times and familiarize yourself with it. Listen and do not sing or hum along. This is your opportunity to simply learn the melody and take it in.

STEP TWO: PRINT LYRICS, MARK BREATHS AND START SINGING

In Step Two, print out the lyrics and mark your breaths, while continuing to listen to the new song. Listen for the natural breathing spots after each phrase within the song and mark them with an apostrophe. Breath is critical in a performance and ensures you are supporting yourself in a way that avoids vocal harm or injury. Once you've marked your breaths, it's time to start singing the song as written and move on to Step Three.

STEP THREE: MEMORIZE AND BEGIN PAINTING

Once you start singing, focus on memorizing the lyrics in chunks. Have a clear understanding of the message behind the lyrics and look for any commonalities or connections between the verses and chorus. You might find a lot of repetition which will take a longer song and make it much easier to memorize.

Identify the driving force and beats that lead to the arc and focus on vocal dynamics that will give "color" or "flavor" to your song. Adding color through vocal tones and shades is a way to offer song expression and create a more appealing listening experience. Color is also another way to make the song uniquely and authentically yours. In this step, if you're confident in your musicianship, you can explore new arrangements that might help you stand out.

STEP FOUR: CONNECT

Step Four is where you "bring the fire" and do the soul connection that leads to a memorable, chair turning, "feeling all the feels" performance. Having an authentic emotional connection conveys your ability as the artist to capture the emotion behind the song, the feeling behind the lyrics and communicate it clearly in a personal way.

Discovering this personal connection to the song, will enhance your performance and make the listener feel as if the song has been yours all along! Why is this important? Because the personal connection you create to the song is the game-changing difference.

This is the connection that will pack a punch, deliver chills across the room and up the judges arms, give a casting director "the feels" and bring an audience to tears, then on to their feet! It will also make you proud to perform the song in a way that's real and authentic to you.

To create the connection, reference The Emotion to Real Life Inventory, an acting technique acquired in my early twenties living the voiceover life in Los Angeles. It simply helps you establish the level of emotion of the creative piece or in this case the song, and assign emotional context to it. Ultimately, the lyrics guide you to identify the emotions within the song.

For example, if the song is about a major heartbreak or devastating break up, how would you relate if you've never been deeply in love? It's quite possible, you've never had your heart completely crushed. Many singers might relate to the heart ache, but if you're one that has never experienced this, you can utilize The Emotion to Real Life Inventory and relate to different levels of emotion.

In this case, you'd relate to a high level of sadness. Can you relate to being let down or intensely frustrated? Can you relate to feeling betrayed? Perhaps you've experienced depression or a deep sadness or loss in the past.

Inside The Emotion to Real Life Inventory, there are high, medium and low levels of emotion. From the lyrics, you will determine the specific emotion your performance needs to convey. Once you identify this emotion, correlate it to a real life story you've experienced. This simple technique will bridge a personal connection to a song you did not write.

To get your free pdf download of the Emotion To Real Life Inventory, scan the QR code below or click here at https://scnv.io/wBBV:

STEP FIVE: PERFORM

In this last step, you bring it all together. You've learned the melody, you've mastered the breath support, you've made the song uniquely yours, and you've created a personal connection. Now it's time to unleash it in a jaw dropping, awe inspiring performance.

Yes! This can be yours. Believe It!

Prior to your performance, channel your inner actor and take yourself back and recall that emotional experience or real life story. Feel it deeply to create that authentic connection again. Bring that intensity and raw emotion to the song at performance time and others will feel it. Express the emotion through your whole body, and allow us to see a real connection through your eyes and hear it in your voice.

The judges, casting director, or listener must know without a doubt, this song means something to you— as you present it in a way that makes them want more and deeply moves them. When you make them **feel** something, that is the difference between being memorable and forgettable. You capture their attention and give them every reason to put you through to the next round.

This is how you take a song you haven't written to that next level and make others believe in you. Be sure to record the emotion and associated story in your journal to recall for a future song that calls for the same emotional connection. Master Steps Four and Five and as you progress inside the competition, and you'll confidently create an authentic connection to any material given to you.

MISTAKE THREE

This last common mistake is one I've mentioned before, but trust me, it bears repeating. Avoid Comparison. On reality singing competitions, all artists are created equal. From the super green, Novice singer, just starting out, to the seasoned Musician performer, each artist brings something unique to the reality party. In most cases, reality singing competitions are full of extremely talented individuals.

"One of the things that was very interesting to me, was meeting other contestants like me: my age, my level, my game. I was at the top with these guys, and they were really, really good. I realized I was not alone and there are other people out there with the same level of thinking and level of talent, who wanted to impact and change the world. It was a very gratifying experience being with others who knew they were there for a bigger purpose."

**—Griffin Holtby, Rock/Blues Artist
American Idol**

As noted in the introduction, reality singing shows attract a versatile group of performers. The Musician contestants might make their way to the show through private audition experiences, while others submit virtual auditions online or apply for in person open calls. Often, these artists who receive a private audition, have attracted a casting director or producer's attention through established social media accounts.

You might assume the Musician who scores a private audition has a leg up because they were invited to audition, but don't forget about the promising Novice, who's hungry to be heard and seen. The Novice is eager to impress and prove they deserve an equal shot at their reality dreams.

Both The Musician and The Novice are competing on a level playing field. So, at the end of the day, remember, **do not fret or expend energy trying to figure out what the judges, casting directors or producers are looking for**. You cannot possibly know what's going on inside their head, therefore, you cannot compare yourself with the Joe next to you. In all circumstances, if one does not fit inside the casting mold for that specific season, they will be sent home to try again next time.

You've now learned three of the most common mistakes contestants make inside reality singing show competitions. Do your best to avoid these pitfalls. In the next chapter, you'll discover the secret that will help you maximize your entire reality singing show experience.

TAKE ACTION:

Write down three success tips you can rely on to you avoid the common mistakes covered in this chapter.

Chapter 10

DEVELOP YOUR AUDITION EDGE

Beyond song choice and your consistent artist vibe, lies a critical and equally important component that will help you edge out your competition. The secret to making a huge impact inside the reality singing show and maximizing the experience is the power of creating a compelling brand story. In this chapter you'll learn how to define your core brand story and develop an audition edge that will set you apart from other strong contenders.

Congratulations! You're on your way to a successful singing competition experience, and guess what? There are vocalists and performers auditioning next to you, that are either equally as good as you, or they're better than you. So what is going to give you that edge for a producer or casting director to choose you over them?

The short answer? Your story. In addition to your interesting personality shining on camera and delivering the full artist package, your voice and your story are equally important. Establishing a core brand story that is relatable, heartfelt and authentic to your experience, is critical prior to the audition process. You must get your story straight before your audition.

So what do I mean by that? Think about any reality tv singing show you've ever watched. Can you recall seeing video packages that give a peek inside the contestant's life? You may have seen an emotional young man, sharing his struggle with depression, or the single mom or dad who loves to sing, but chose their family over music. Every story offers a personal, emotional connection and gives the viewers a reason to root them on.

You don't need a sad story to craft your core brand story. You simply need a process to create and share your unique perspective on life. Above all, you must be vulnerable; however, determine in advance what you're comfortable sharing. It is very important that you do not overshare if you're not healed. Revealing the inner workings of a broken relationship or traumatic event, before it's fully behind you, can be destructive and cause more harm than good.

Your core brand story is true and authentic to you. You'll design this message to impact others and make a positive difference in the world. If you're not ready to divulge a deeper part of your personal story to the world, and the millions of people who are going to see your story on television, be very clear and intent on preserving it. It's acceptable to keep some things private.

Part of your story may highlight a positive thing that has come from an awful experience, showing how you went from pain to promise. You might acknowledge that sure, it still hurts, but you're healed, your whole and you now have hope out of this dark situation. Through your story, you can inspire belief in others. If you're not ready to share that dark story, find something else. You are more than your past and your future is waiting to be designed.

Keep in mind, once you progress to later rounds inside the competition, many shows will require psychological testing to ensure you're emotionally healthy and stable. So before you enter this audition experience, ask yourself, "can I handle this competition on an emotional level," and if so ask, "what am I comfortable sharing?" Also identify what you're **not** comfortable sharing. Both are equally important.

"You want to have mental peace with sharing your story. It will go out to millions of people and you'll not only get positive feedback, but you'll also get negative feedback as well. If you're not at peace with sharing your story to millions without caring what they think, don't share it."

**—Jo James, Neo-Soul Artist,
The Voice Season 17**

The ability to express your core brand story in a clear and consistent way, will set you apart from the other contestants. It will also give the show compelling content and give you the best opportunity to be featured on an artist highlight package before your audition airs. Acquiring this footage is a huge step to maximizing the reality singing show platform, because your story is what cultivates a real relationship between you and your fans.

Please do not make the same mistake I did during my audition for American Idol. When they asked me, "so who are you? Can you tell us a little bit about yourself?" I responded by reciting my entire high school and college resume, which was not interesting at all. I was rattling off facts of my life versus sharing stories that make people feel.

We've touched on this inside previous chapters, but what happens when you make people feel something? That's right! You become memorable. You make an impact!

Take it from Sales 101. Facts tell, stories sell, so stop spitting out facts in your attempt to explain who you are, and instead share through a story. When you craft your story, take the time to practice communicating your message in a clear and concise manner. Remember, there is only one you, and you have a unique perspective on life to share.

No one owns your story except for you, which is why your story is your edge. Take the time to get it straight. In this chapter, you learned the importance of delivering your core brand story in a concise, authentic way. Remember, your story is equally, if not more important than you having an impeccable singing voice.

Now that you have all your audition arsenal in place, it's time to get amped up! In the next chapter, you'll take all the preparation and put it to use on your big Audition Day! For now, grab your journal and work through the questions below to get started on your Personal Core Brand Story.

Once you've formulated your story, take it a step further and say it aloud. Practice communicating your story effectively and consistently, until it flows naturally.

TAKE ACTION:

1. How did you get started? What were your challenges or struggles along the way that defined your path today and how old were you?

2. What challenge(s) held you back and what change did you want to make?

3. What happened to make you realize you could actually make a change?

4. How can your journey offer hope and inspiration to others?

Section four

TIME TO SHINE

DESIGN YOUR CHAIR TURNING
AUDITION DAY GAME PLAN

Chapter 11

BE UNSTOPPABLE

You've been preparing for months, have your vocal chops in tip-top shape and are hyper clear on your creative brand. You're able to communicate a compelling brand story with ease, and you feel ready to impress the judges.

Producers call your name and then it hits. The butterflies start swelling in the pit of your stomach. You begin to sweat and panic and now you've forgotten your lyrics and all of your "back pocket" songs. Suddenly, the extensive preparation leading up to this point has been forgotten and you begin to doubt you're even good enough to be there.

This doesn't have to be your outcome. Channel your inner warrior and take a deep breath. Allow your nerves to serve as an indication that you're alive and take control of that energy by imagining the immense feeling of joy and pride you'll have, once you knock your audition out of the park.

In this chapter, you'll master your audition day mindset and create an unstoppable game day performance plan. Your positive, focused mindset, provides a plan with "go-time" ammunition to make your big impression and avoid self-sabotage. Ultimately, you have the power over your mind to change your negative thought patterns and create a positive outcome.

ADJUST YOUR PHYSICALITY

Try a physical response or something new when your nerves start presenting themselves. Acknowledge the fear mentally, flip the switch, and disrupt the pattern by physically moving your body to pump yourself up. This might look like you doing jumping jacks, throwing a fists pump in the air, shaking out your wrists, clapping or saying a loud, firm "yes, I got this! Boom!" (That's personally my favorite)

"It's not about being "ready". You need to be UNSTOPPABLE!! Any emotion you're feeling is based on how you're moving. Little movements like breathing and big movements like gestures and facial expressions. Discover how you can use your body to immediately direct your mind and your emotions."

—Tony Robbins, #1 Life & Business Strategist, Entrepreneur, Personal Power

Don't worry about looking ridiculous. You have arrived at your audition and this your opportunity to slay the judges and in order for you to perform at your top, not only must you believe it's possible, but you must control your focus from the nerves, to a feeling of power. This can be achieved through a physical response that tells your body, "I'm here to rock my audition and I'm doing it now!"

Getting out of your comfort zone is growth and when you're growing, it's uncomfortable. Embrace the discomfort and keep pressing because you're here to deliver the goods. Tap into your WHY and execute everything you've been working on.

When you choose to lean into your fear versus cowering under it, you open yourself to the opportunity on the other side. Remember everything you've learned leading up to this point and that in order for the judges to have fun, you must be having fun. Let your personality shine and deliver an engaging, interesting, entertaining audition performance. Show the producers and judges, you're excited to be there.

"You are not unique in your fear as everyone has experienced it on some level. Taking risks and getting out of your comfort zone isn't a perfect process, so mistakes or even failure are inevitable. Acknowledge your fear and send it packing."

—Performing Artist Pathway

COMBAT NEGATIVE SELF-TALK AND SELF-SABOTAGE

Your job is to walk into the audition room with confidence, show them your stuff, have fun, smile, and kick butt. Your job is not to compare yourself to the talent around you or over analyze what the judges are looking for. Get out of your head and remove the negative self-talk in order to focus on performing at your highest level. When you get caught up in everybody else's business around you, you open yourself up to be knocked off your game.

Comparison robs joy, so even if you think the contestant next to you has the best voice you've ever heard in your life and you're questioning, "Oh my Goodness. If they don't make it, how in the heck am I going to make it?" Remember you bring something unique to the table and you can't compare apples to oranges. Get yourself out on the audition stage and perform at a hundred percent.

Prepare for the nerves and create your plan for an unstoppable performance. Take yourself back to a time where you felt nervous. What lies were you hearing in your head? What chatter was going on that paralyzed you from performing at your best? Take your journal out and record the negative self-talk, then next to it, create a truth statement that counters the lie. Acknowledges your strengths and positive beliefs you have for yourself.

Make a record of all the amazing things you are excited about and proud of in your life. Commit these to memory, so when self doubt and self sabotage pop up, you have an arsenal of self-belief and self-love to combat it. Also record some physical moves you can do that will interrupt the nerves and shift your focus to confidence in your audition.

ADJUST THE EXPECTATION

Although it's easy to place an immense amount of pressure and expectation on yourself, fight the urge to wrap your worth into the outcome of your audition. This is only the beginning and your participation alone will serve as a learning experience to grow from.

"When we put a lot of pressure on ourselves, we don't show up and we don't give the best performance that we want to give. So think of it this way, even if it doesn't work out according to your expectations, that doesn't mean that it was a failure. That doesn't mean it didn't work out.

Open yourself up to all of the possibilities, because there are a million ways this could go. No matter the outcome, it will end up being for the best down the line, whether it opens you up to other opportunities that are a better fit, or whether a producer calls you back a couple months later for a different opportunity. Everything happens for a reason and what is for you shall not pass."

—Katie Zaccardi, Holistic Music Career Coach.

There's a lot in the phrase "perfect timing," because whether or not this opportunity works out in the exact fashion you're anticipating, you can trust all is as it should be. Don't put a timeline on your success or a timestamp on when you think it should all happen. Are you really in control of that? I tried three times before I got the "Yes!" If I would've stopped at my second audition, I would've never had the privilege of making the show to begin with.

Take action and open yourself up to receiving opportunities in their perfect time, not **your** perfect time. Not everything is about you. Don't limit or restrict the goodness coming your way, simply because your expectations aren't being met in the way you planned them in your head.

This chapter has empowered you to begin forming your personal arsenal to combat any negativity that tries to interfere with your unstoppable audition performance. You learned that you are capable and you are prepared. In the next chapter, you'll learn what it takes to create a chair turning, "YES!" moment that will propel you to the next round!

TAKE ACTION:

1. Create a positive MENTAL association and think about how you'll FEEL when you have an amazing audition. Have a mantra or positive affirmation prepared and commit it to memory. Something confident and empowering like "I Can & I Will Handle This."

2. Record your strengths and gifts and keep them handy to help you combat negative self talk.

3. Create a PHYSICAL action or power move to get you amped up and full of energy for your big opportunity. Think about what you naturally do when you're excited. (ie: Fist Pump, Double fists in the air, confident strut, hand clap, boom!)

Chapter 12

GIVE THEM NO OPTION, BUT TO SAY, "YES!"

You've personally done this a hundred times. From the couch, you intently study a contestant's audition while watching your favorite reality singing show. You inadvertently put yourself in the judge's shoes and suddenly, think, "are they ready? Are they good enough to move to the next level of the competition? Did they choose the right song and are they giving me enough to say "YES! You Belong On This Show!"

Newsflash, you're not the judge, but you are being judged the minute you enter the audition room. In this chapter, you'll learn how to create that "Yes! We want you!" moment and slay your live audition.

When you're making an impression with producers, casting directors or judges, there are several best practices you can develop to make a strong first impression on audition day. The moment you walk onto the audition stage, you're being judged. From your appearance to your posture, confidence, and of course, your voice and stage performance. Set yourself up for success, so you can deliver the best you can.

STAGE PRESENCE

Something as simple as a hunched back or fidgety hands, can convey a lack of preparation and confidence and immediately send the wrong message. This is all before you've opened your mouth to deliver your song. So if you enter the stage hunched over and uneasy, the decision makers will feel your nerves and potentially experience nerves as well! Radiate confidence upon entrance and be laser focused on what you're there to do.

Most importantly, have fun, because if you lack control of your nerves, you'll lose your ability to showcase your personality and talent, making it very difficult to get cast. Loosen up and demonstrate your confidence right out of the gate. Introduce yourself with ease and imagine talking to your best friend, but kick up the politeness a bit. Communicating naturally is the key to showing off your authenticity.

This is when you must show off both your artist brand vibe and your personality. Ultimately, they're not just casting your voice, they're casting you as a person.

You're becoming a potential cast member for their product: an entertainment television show. Bring the excitement, be captivating, and grab their attention.

Producers, casting directors and judges are looking for the complete package: the personality, the swagger, the talent, the look. Present yourself in a way that makes them think, "I can't live without this person. They have to be on my show!" Leave it all on the stage, so when you walk away, you can rest assured without regret, you delivered your absolute best.

MUSICIANSHIP AND ENERGY

If you're used to accompanying yourself with an instrument like guitar or piano, practice, with and without that instrument. If you make it on the show, producers will ask you to perform without it, and if you're not prepared, this could mess with your performance mojo, because you might feel "naked" on stage without your instrument. Whether performing acapella or with accompaniment, judges will be looking for accurate pitch, nice tone, and they'll want to hear *you*, so be sure to project with or without your instrument.

Recall what you learned in Chapter Nine through The Emotion To Real Life Inventory. You've connected to your audition material in a real, authentic way, and this reflects through your eyes and body energy. Eye contact is crucial during your song delivery because it not only communicates confidence, but it unveils the deep connection you have to the music. If you close your eyes the entire song, it blocks that connection and diminishes the impact of the emotion you are trying to convey.

It is not necessary to stare the judges down, because this might be uncomfortable for everyone, but use the simple trick of looking past or through them, or shifting your focus to their cheek, or forehead. Your ability to connect and deliver the emotion of the song in a compelling way is what inspires the producers and judges to feel the intensity. If they aren't watching you, they will still hear the fire in your voice and feel it through your energy.

One way to create an awareness of your live performance habits is through a video. Take some footage of yourself and pretend you're in a live audition scenario. Start with your introduction and move into the performance of your song. Pay close attention to your eye contact, your hand and arm movement, your posture and body positioning and overall energy. Are you effectively communicating the emotion of the song in a powerful way? Do you sound natural when you introduce yourself or does it feel scripted?

Remember, if you're not right for this show or this season, you're still making an impression that could pay off in the long run. You might get a call six months from now from someone in casting saying, "Hey, you auditioned for *The Voice*. You weren't right for that season, but I want you to come back and audition for the next." So you're not only auditioning for this opportunity, but you could very well be auditioning for a future opportunity as well.

Ultimately, to get to the "YES!," you must make people feel deeply connected to you and this chapter drove home the gravity of delivering a powerful audition that makes people feel. Take action now to create your own video audition and record your discoveries in your journal. In the next chapter, you'll begin to look at the many ways you can maximize your reality singing show experience and build connections that will transcend long after your time on the show is up.

Section five

IT'S ALL ABOUT
THE SPRINGBOARD, BABY

LEVERAGE THE PLATFORM AS A
LAUNCHPAD FOR YOUR MUSIC CAREER

Chapter 13

SQUEEZE THAT JUICE

Project ahead with me as we move into this final section. You've made it on the show or you've made it to the next round, congratulations! Whether it's to Hollywood or the Top 20, you'll have great success on and off the show if you learn to squeeze the most juice out of this experience. In this chapter, you'll learn what to expect once you make the show and the power of connecting to build momentum in your music career.

The ride just got a little more interesting, and it's time to play the game and show up strong. When you make it to this level of the reality singing competition, prove that you belong there and give it your absolute best. Resist any urge you might have to hold back, out of fear of protecting yourself. Now is **not** the time to hold back. It is the time to **unleash**!

Protecting your heart from pain is a natural desire. It's also common to convince yourself that what you've accomplished up to this point is enough. But is it really "enough?" Are you satisfied with not trying to take your talent as far as it can possibly go? Let me take a moment to caution you against this negative thought process. If you approach your remaining time on the show, acting like you don't care, you might as well start packing your bags.

There will be other contestants who aren't satisfied with "enough" or a mediocre performance and who will demonstrate how hungry they are to succeed. That's what you're up against, so if you're ready to throw in the towel, because you don't want your ego crushed, then put down this book right now and stop wasting your time. Or, you can challenge yourself to flip the script and show that you truly care.

The truth is, I want you to care and I want you to take a risk at getting hurt. I want you to risk feeling rejected, because without risk, there is no reward. The energy and love you put in is what you'll receive right back. As in life, when you put in the negative, you reap the negative, and I don't want that for you. You've come too far to throw it all away now. So choose to move into the next phase of this competition, in a positive way so that you can get the most of it.

"Competition feels like the worst place to be as a creative, but it's worth the reward. I overthought every little thing the first time I went through the audition process in Season 13. I enjoyed the ride so much more in Season 17 because I knew what to expect and I realized so much was out of my control. Take in everything you can and use it as fuel for when you either make it further, or you move on once the show has ended!"

**—Matt New, Pop Artist,
The Voice Season 13 & 17**

WHAT TO EXPECT: LEGAL STUFF

When you start progressing through the different stages of the competition, one thing you can expect is mandatory contracts and non-disclosure agreements to protect confidentiality. Some shows hire lawyers to help you understand the terms of each contract, negotiate when possible and ensure that you're keeping your best interests in mind. Contracts can be overwhelming, so if you have the means to hire a music industry lawyer, you might want to consider it.

"It's one thing to know what you want to do when there's no doors opening. It's a whole other thing, when you have a hundred doors open, to know which one's the right door. When the doors start flying open, then the reality sets in, "do I really know what I want?"""

—Cas Haley, Texas Singer-Songwriter-Guitarist, America's Got Talent Season 2 Runner Up

Once you make the show, and depending on how far you take it, you will be legally obligated to confidentiality for a certain period of time and bound to the rules of the show. In many cases, you could be bound to the show for at least 6 months after the last air date. Keep this in mind if you're planning to release new music or have already committed yourself to any large work projects. Based on your priorities, you'll have to decide whether to release the music later, push the project or simply audition for the show another season. Be aware of your legal responsibilities and plan accordingly.

WHAT TO EXPECT: LOTS OF INFORMATION

Another thing to expect is a lot of email correspondence communicating clear expectations on what to prepare or what to know prior to coming on the show. But here's the kicker... often, this information is not communicated in one email, nor is it on the timeline you think it should be. There might be some waiting involved, so It's very important you don't overlook the different emails from the show on general logistics, music, wardrobe and travel.

Pay attention to specifically what they are asking for and respond accordingly. Another thing that may not seem like a big deal to you, is understanding the days, times and locations of where they want you to be. If for some reason they're not giving you that information, follow up with your contact at the show and request specific details. Create best practices for yourself and take ownership of where you need to be and when you need to be there.

Don't make the same grave mistake I did, leading up to my Hollywood audition round. As I shared with you in Chapter Two, I didn't communicate with the show to let them know I had moved and my contestant packet was sent to an old address. I made an incorrect assumption I had all the information needed to prepare for Hollywood. The material I'd been diligently practicing on with my vocal coach for an entire month, was never put to use. Be aware that it's on **you** to ensure you have the accurate information.

WHAT TO EXPECT:
LONG DAYS AND LATE NIGHTS

Inside the show, remember to keep things consistent. Arrive with awesome energy every single day and give it everything you got. There will be long hours, sleep deprivation and conditions that are not ideal for your singing voice. Luckily the adrenaline will be surging through you, but be aware that this schedule can take a toll on your body.

"Once you make it on the show, the schedule, pressure, lack of sleep and the waiting around make the experience pure insanity. There were times when we waited for hours, trying to stay warmed up and ready to rock 'n roll. It was just crazy and it was really tough trying to "stay ready" and bring your best game after having to wait so long."

**—Tori Martin, Country Artist,
American Idol Season 14**

Outside variables can knock you off your game. Recall everything you did to prepare mentally, physically and vocally, leading up to the show. All of these will help sustain your energy and mindset through the process. Although you worked diligently on these, there will still be pressures you're not anticipating.

Steer clear of drama between other contestants and do your best to have fun and continue showing off your personality. As an entertainment television show, the intensity will be kicked up because it makes for good TV. Be flexible when you receive last minute information from production on any changes they are making. Remember, you are not the only contestant on the show that will have to adjust. Everyone is in the same boat. Awareness is the key.

WHAT TO EXPECT: WARDROBE AND MAKEUP

Looking your best in front of the cameras is extremely important when marketing your artist brand. Reality singing shows have departments for wardrobe and makeup that will help ensure you're looking great.

Pay close attention to the guidelines provided to you from the wardrobe department concerning what to wear or what not to wear. In most cases, you will bring your own outfits for consideration. The wardrobe department may use some of the clothing you brought, combined with some of their own clothing, or give you a completely new look all together.

When it comes to show time, wardrobe will guide the style choices, but producers typically have the final say in what you will wear. Keep in mind, reality singing shows vary, so be prepared to bring your best look that represents you as an artist, and trust you will make an impression.

MAKEUP

Whether you're a fan of makeup or not, get ready to experience it in a new way. Production lights have a tendency to wash you out and they get hot, so proper makeup is essential in order for you to show up well on camera. Creative Brand Expert Meagan D'von Funk has spent a lot of time working on sets and provides her top tips on makeup:

"People react to nerves and high pressure situations differently. Most often they sweat. Even the ones that don't typically sweat. Keep a towel nearby. Theater makeup is great to research because they have products, to prep the skin, that will reduce or stop excessive sweating. Contrary to common belief, both men and women need makeup for on-camera appearances. Look specifically for a matte powder with no shimmer or shine in it. MAC Studio Fix Powder Foundation is my superstar television product. It is available in a great range of colors, controls oil and the buildable coverage works well alone or with other products."

—Meagan D'Von Funk, Creative Consultant & Director of Loft Stories

LIGHTS, CAMERA, ACTION! IT'S TIME TO CONNECT!

It's time to connect! Make it a habit to connect with your production crew. When you're kind to the crew, they'll be kind to you. Prepare for the cameras, the crews and the commotion, because if you're not used to being filmed, it can feel pretty awkward and uncomfortable. You'll be mic'd up and there will be cameras everywhere, so be aware of the words that come out of your mouth. You have granted the show permission to use everything!

When you're on set, they're capturing everything you say, even if you're not directly mic'd. So imagine having a conversation with another contestant, and you don't think they're catching any of your conversation. Think again and understand that the things you say, or the quirky things you do, could be at some point edited for inclusion in montages and general entertainment purposes.

"No one is out to make someone look bad, because the more the contestants experience success, the more money everyone makes in the long run. All of these competition shows would love to have 10+ singers leaving the show, releasing music and having massive success, because it reflects well on the show."

—Jonathon Ragsdale, Online Editor
American Idol, 11 Seasons

The second group you want to connect with are the judges. You won't always get the opportunity to network with them *per se*, but develop your connection from the stage. Show off your personality and confidence, but stay true to who you are and exercise humility. When you connect from the stage, remember to deliver your performance through the eyes and full body, so the judges and cameras feel your energy.

Lastly, connect and network inside the show with contestants, crew members and coaches. This is the ultimate opportunity to leverage the power of relationships and will be one of the biggest resources you can use to maximize your experience on this reality singing show. Whether you're an introvert or social butterfly, make the effort to form authentic relationships with others inside the show.

The more you're out and about talking with others on the show, the more opportunities there are to get screen time as well. At this stage in the game, you want people to know who you are and you want the opportunity to share your story. Use this networking arena to grow your social media following and collect contact information from other contestants. You never know when one of these new relationships will turn into a future collaboration.

Creating connections is one of the great perks of being on a reality singing show. Relationships lead to opportunities to share your music, your artist brand, message, and story. Creating long term connections, whether it be with executive producers, contestants, production crew, or even professional musicians and vocal coaches inside this show, is a big way to leverage your competition experience. These meaningful relationships will also serve you in the long game of your music career.

In this chapter, you learned what to expect inside the show and how connecting with others can lead to great relationships long after the season has ended. Coming up, you'll identify more ways you can maximize any exposure you get on television, to grow your fan base, and create real momentum in your music career.

Chapter 14

BE A BOSS

Performance, networking and creating music are all very exciting components inside the life of any performing artist. The business side, marketing and strategy, however can often feel overwhelming. In this chapter, you will learn three top business foundations to focus on, so you can be the boss of your music career and prepare for the future growth of your fan base.

Imagine for a moment having the opportunity to share your talent with millions, who will hear your story, your message and your music. There is a real possibility that **millions** of eyes and ears could catch your audition or watch your story package, if you get featured on a reality singing show. That exposure increases every time you progress to a new stage of the competition. So when that happens to you, and there are millions checking you out on social media or searching your name in Google, what will they discover?

If you want to truly maximize this opportunity, it's critical you get your ducks in a row, and get all of your music business foundation pieces intact. This will best position you to connect with the millions of potential new fans discovering you for the first time. The three business foundation areas I recommend you focusing on **before** your reality singing show debut are: your social media presence, website or landing page, and email list.

SOCIAL MEDIA PRESENCE

When someone searches for you on social media, what do they see? Is your feed flooded with pictures of your cat or crazy photos with you and your friends? Establishing a consistent brand message and music-centric social media presence, prior to getting on a reality singing show, is very important. This starts by having an official public Business account or Creator account versus a personal one.

A business profile gives you more access to connecting with your fans, such as insights on who your followers are, where they live, and when they are most often tuning in on social media. This can lead to optimum engagement as you tailor your messaging to your audience, and also learn the best times to post. Your business profile will also track analytics, collect data, and enable you to target your followers with paid ads when you're ready.

Take advantage of your ability to create an efficient profile link. Many artists underutilize the ability to provide a website link in their profile, or assume if they don't have a website, there is nothing to share. This is far beyond the truth and you have many options to create opportunities to engage with your followers.

Platforms like Campsite.bio, ContactInBio.com or Linktr.ee are there to help you optimize the single profile link you can provide on your social media accounts. There are many helpful free and paid features you can get from these platforms, that will allow you to promote multiple projects. This link will also drive traffic to your website and collect email addresses when set up properly. Some of the PRO accounts allow you to integrate a Facebook Pixel—a tool that tracks data from visitors to your profile link— so you can market your music or products to them down the road using Facebook Ads.

As you attract new fans, visitors and followers to your social media profile, I recommend optimizing your link to include the following:

- Your Website or Landing Page if available (equipped with a Facebook Tracking Pixel)

- A Link To Sign Up for Your Email List (Landing Page or Email Collector Form)

- Links To Your Live Performances or Music Videos

- Links To Any Music Fans Can Stream Or Download

- Links to any Press or Social Proof

While on the show, you will be unable to share a lot of your content concerning your experience, due to contracts and confidentiality. But, take this opportunity and collect content throughout your reality show experience. Once the show ends and you have the green light, you'll be able to start sharing more, and dripping out the content to release it slowly.

Another crucial component you want to have for your social media accounts **before** you get on a reality singing show is a cohesive brand aesthetic. If you're just getting started with social media or you've been neglecting your account for a while, start by ensuring your profile picture, photos inside your feed and messaging represent you as an artist. Remove or archive any content that is irrelevant or inappropriate.

Create an interesting profile description that gives new visitors a very clear idea of who you are as an artist and what they'll get when they follow you. If your goal is to attract a reality tv casting producer, include your age and where you live, to help them determine whether you're eligible for their show.

Update all social media platforms with the same profile picture, banners and descriptions to create brand continuity and eliminate any confusion. Keep in mind, it is not necessary for you to be on every single platform. Think about where your followers spend most of their time and stick to platforms you can do well. Lastly, design a content plan for your social media, so you can create consistency in your brand message.

REPRESENTATION ON MUSIC PLATFORMS

If you have original music released already or have been doing live shows for a while, chances are you have your music on platforms like YouTube, Spotify or iTunes. Just as you created brand continuity on your social media platforms, you should do the same on your music platforms. Also ensure that the music videos and content that you've already released are quality sound and visual recordings.

Quality content is extremely important to create trust and also leads to monetization of your music. Creating great music can attract inclusion on Spotify playlists that can lead to additional streams and earning more. On YouTube, it can increase your subscriber count, and when you hit 1000 subscribers, you become eligible to start earning money there as well. Lastly, if you have music available for purchase on platforms such as iTunes or Amazon, and your new fans and followers discover that, it could lead to downloads and charting, creating more traction and visibility on your music.

YOUR DIGITAL FOOTPRINT

If you create a professional online presence for yourself and have web authority, not only will you be searchable, but you will create credibility for yourself and inspire new fans to hop on board your music journey. It's critical to create multiple avenues for you to stay connected with your new fans, once the show is behind you. Websites and landing pages are one way for you to track your visitors and invite them into your music fold.

Establishing domain or web authority is another reason why it's important to create a website or landing page prior to your reality singing show experience. Web authority, outside of social media platforms increases your digital footprint and searchability.

Take the time to learn more about the advantages of utilizing Facebook pixels. Facebook pixels allow you to track your visitors, when your specific pixel code is placed on your website. The code collects data that helps you track conversions from Facebook ads, optimize ads, build targeted audiences for future ads, and remarket to people who have already taken some kind of action on your website.

Your new visitors are likely to be on Facebook or Instagram, so adding this code to your website or landing page is a great way to reach these fresh fans in the future. Social media platforms are constantly evolving, so it's important to stay on top of the most recent changes. If you're creating a Facebook pixel code for the first time, be sure to visit the Business Help Center inside Facebook, to get the most up to date information on how to set this up.

THE POWER OF EMAIL

As previously mentioned, you're about to capture the attention of millions of people. Millions of eyes and ears will be on you, so what happens when they follow you on social media? What's your plan to capture their data and information to ensure your ability to keep in touch. Tracking through facebook pixels is one way, but there's something that will help you get even more targeted.

The last and possibly most important component you want to have in place **before** you go on a reality singing show is an Email List. Your list could consist of two people: You and your best friend. The priority is to have the list created, so that you can add to it once you expand your impact.

Your reality singing show experience will provide a great advantage of gaining new exposure and increasing your fan base. Collecting emails is one powerful way to leverage the experience, so you can stay in touch, nurture new fan relationships and ultimately, create a thriving community of followers who want to support your music career.

I'm a big advocate for having multiple streams of communication, so when you couple social media with email, you've got a winning combination. Numbers don't lie, so if you're a statistics person, you'll appreciate these from Campaign Monitor on email and social media respectively:

- There are 3x more email accounts than there are Facebook, Instagram & Twitter accounts.

- Organic (free) reach (i.e., the number of your fans who actually see your posts without having to pay for ads) has shrunk to 1-2% on Facebook and Instagram over the past two years.

- On the contrary, open rates for email marketing messages are in the 20-30% range, which means that your email is over 10x more likely to be seen through email versus social media.

- Lastly, click through rates for email are in the 3% range vs the .5% range on social media, which means the next time you're launching new music or new merchandise, you're 6x more likely to get a download or purchase through email.

Above all, the most powerful reason for starting your email list is the sheer fact that you own your list. Powerhouse social media platforms like Facebook and

Instagram can come and go and you could lose all your precious followers. Or your account could get hacked, heaven forbid. Email marketing platforms make it easy to download and store your email list on a consistent basis to keep your contacts safe.

So many contestants miss the opportunity to capture the information from their new followers because they don't have a system in place. Don't miss out on yours. Create your list before going on the show, so you're prepared for the future growth of your fan base. When you do, you'll position yourself to connect intentionally and cultivate true fan relationships long after the show is over.

COLLECTING EMAIL

Now that you understand the benefits of having an email list, where's the best place to start? First choose an email marketing platform to collect and store your email addresses. I recommend starting with Mailchimp because they're the global leader in email marketing, have a robust list of free offerings and integrate seamlessly with other platforms. Mailchimp also makes it very simple to collect, store and organize your email contacts. They do not, however, have the monopoly on email marketing platforms, so do your research and choose one that best suits your needs.

Next, start collecting email addresses from fans and followers. It is now easier than ever and there are many ways you can collect email without feeling weird or creepy. The most effective way I recommend is through your website or landing page that can integrate with your email marketing platform.

If you don't have a website that is perfectly fine. Through your email marketing platform of choice , you can create a basic, simple landing page that has your picture, a short bio and links to your music. The landing page will also enable you to add your facebook pixel for tracking and an email collector form to grow your list. Be sure to include at minimum two fields: Email address and First Name. If you'd like to include more, you can make them optional. These two fields are all you need to personalize your communication, thank them for following you, and let them know how they can keep in touch with you.

Email is the best way for new fans to get the inside scoop on your journey, and how they can support you in your music career. Entice them to sign up by offering something they'd appreciate, like a free download of an unreleased or exclusive acoustic song. Get creative and also deliver something to your fans that they can easily access through email. Once your fan signs up, you'll be able to utilize the automation features inside your email platform, automate a response thanking them, and also provide the freebie promised.

Other ways to collect email is through a pro option on a platform like Linktr.ee or through a simple auto response in Messenger or Direct Message. A pro option in Linktr.ee, will allow you in a single button, to collect a visitors email address. The only downside to a platform like this, is the inability to collect a first name and personalize your communication with them. A more personal, grassroots approach, would be to send a direct message every time you get a new follower and invite them to sign up.

That message could look something like this:

"Hey <NAME!>

Thanks for the follow, it means a lot. It's really important to me to keep in touch with my fans because this music journey is a lot more fun when others come along! Would love to invite you to be a part of my music insider crew. You can join the party here <insert landing page link to email collector form> and I'll even send you an exclusive acoustic download of one of my favorite songs <insert your freebie of choice>! See you on the inside!"

Customize the above to suit your voice, but ultimately, give them the opportunity to "become an insider," stay in the know, and be a part of your journey. Remember, fans can't support your music career when you don't invite them into your music fold.

There are several avenues for using the reality singing show platform to expand your music impact. In this chapter, you learned to be the Boss of your music career through a professional social media presence, web authority, and a system to collect email. Having a smart, intentional plan for creating long lasting success is the best way to maximize the reality singing show platform. In the next chapter, you'll discover an exit plan that will give you the best chance for an on-air feature.

Chapter 15

A BEGINNING, NOT AN END

Wherever your journey takes you during this reality singing show experience—at some point—your journey will end. For most, it will end before they hoped, but the most important thing you can do is preserve your relationship with the show and depart gracefully. In this chapter, you'll learn how to create your best response when your time on the show ends and celebrate the opportunities that lie ahead.

There are two different responses you can take when your time on the show has come to an end:

1. Give sincere thanks and appreciate the opportunity.

2. Lose your temper and act ungrateful.

Don't make the mistake of storming off in a rage, ignoring show producers and camera crew requests for a post interview, or bad mouthing the show. Be gracious and appreciative of the opportunity you had, which you signed up for by the way, and project an attitude of gratitude.

When you express appreciation and say, thank you, you're also going to have a much better chance of getting air time or that feature, which is part of the goal. The air time gives you that opportunity to share your voice and message to potential new fans, so don't jeopardize that opportunity by not controlling your frustration.

REJECTION AND REGRET

As I mentioned above, there will be an ending to this journey and for many of you, it will end in rejection. So I want to dive into the importance of perspective and really identifying first, that you have a lot to celebrate! Making it to the initial casting round, is cause for celebration alone. You successfully caught the eye of casting directors, got yourself in front of producers and opened yourself up to a great opportunity to expand in your personal and professional career.

A lot of times, getting rejected feels incredibly sudden. You've built so much expectation for the experience and suddenly it's over and done with in a blink and you're devastated. You wrap your sense of self worth in an experience, but the truth is, rejection is a **feeling**, not a **being**. It is a limiting state that does not dictate who you are or where you're going in life. You have the choice to learn from the situation and allow it to give you wings!

This is a beginning, not an end. If you're upset because you put all your eggs in one basket, thinking this opportunity is the final straw or the last opportunity you have for a successful music career, think again. This reality show is a launchpad for you to create future success on your terms.

Take it from me. I falsely believed for years that I would never have a career in music after my short stint on American Idol. I had no idea that this simple experience would lead to me becoming a performance coach, an author, podcaster, online course creator and artist consultant. It has also fueled me to continue collaborating with others as a singer-songwriter.

You're headed towards the tip of the iceberg that will propel you towards the rest of your life in music! When you implement the strategies I shared in the previous chapters, which include taking advantage of the networking opportunities, making sure your business is optimized and leveraging the competition as a springboard for your career, you're bound for music success.

Timing is everything and it's natural to have regret. It's natural to think, coulda, shoulda, woulda. "I wish I would've chosen a different song or I wish I would've prepared better." When you live in the past, you prevent yourself from receiving all the awesome opportunities coming your way. Brooding and perpetual focus on the "what ifs" is counter productive. Instead, try to accept it's simply part of your story and allow your story to empower you. Shift your focus onto a new question like, "how can I use this experience to propel me forward?"

Rejection is part of the entertainment industry game. It's an opportunity for you to develop grit, persevere, and ultimately be shaped and refined into the human being you're supposed to be. Evolve through this experience and allow the show's ending to create a new beginning.

MOVING ON AND MOVING UP!

Celebrate! You've come a long way and you'll continue to do amazing things. Keep your self-belief in check, maintain your positive energy and visualize yourself realizing success. Cast fear to the side and be steadfast in the truth that your unique message and story is meant to be shared. You have new fans to connect with, so don't let regret and rejection hold you up!

Once you get the green light from the show—releasing you from your obligations—you can put a plan in place to schedule posts and start sharing content you've been collecting for months. Do not release ten posts in a row of your experience. Drip the content out slowly, and mix it up with other unrelated posts. Continue sharing your experience over the three to six month span proceeding your exit, but keep in mind to stay within your contractual obligations.

Track your growth on social media and get into the habit of responding to posts and comments to create a healthy engagement habit. Take the time to connect with all your new followers to create a real artist to fan relationship and don't forget to invite them to your free music offer, so you can keep in touch.

Lastly, always remember, if you don't succeed, try, try again. You never know the doors this will open up. When you seek opportunities and focus on creating an amazing life for yourself, amazing growth will present itself. So go "Be A Boss" and take your music career in your own hands. You got this and I'm rooting for you every step of the way!

Chapter 16

YOUR INVITATION

Congratulations! You've made it to the end, but don't stop here! This is just the beginning of your journey to music success and I'd love to support you more! If you're ready to make the choice to level up your reality game, I'd love to invite you to check out new ways to maximize your music career.

My first invitation to you, is to join my membership community! Connect with a Community of Reality Show hopefuls and past contestants to get more support inside your reality tv experience and beyond! Get your Membership to the **Reality TV Music Mastermind Facebook Group** today and be sure to let me know you discovered the group from this book!

Your annual membership to the Make Reality TV Your Reality Mastermind group includes:

- Live Q&A Support Sessions Inside The Group With Brianna.

- Exclusive Monthly Expert Trainings on Relevant Topics to Empower You for your Reality Singing Show Experience & Beyond.

- Networking & Support with other reality singing show hopefuls and past contestants.

- Accountability & Massive Energy To Ignite Your Music Journey!

- Access to Mastermind Promos and Discounts.

PLEASE LEAVE A REVIEW

My friend, thank you so much for choosing to spend your time and energy with me, reading this book! I hope you enjoyed it!

But please don't keep your experience a secret. Let others hear about it! I would love your feedback, so please start by leaving a review on Amazon and let me know how this book impacted you and/or your reality singing show experience. Great reviews help others discover the book and also encourage more great reviews, so help me spread this impact by leaving your review today!

Thank you in advance!

GET MORE SUPPORT FROM BRIANNA AND HER TEAM

If you'd like to dive deeper and enroll in the Make Reality TV Your Reality Online Experience, find out more through the link below and join the program today! Just for being a reader, you'll get $100 OFF when you use promo code **BOOK100** at checkout!

Make Reality TV Your Reality Online Experience Includes:

- Self-paced online course including full access to video trainings, resources and worksheets, to position you to maximize your reality singing show experience.

- In depth interviews with music industry experts and past reality show contestants, offering additional insight into how to prepare for the show!

- Coaching: 1:1 Package with Brianna to Supercharge Your Next Audition!

- Community: One Year Membership to the Make Reality TV Your Reality Mastermind Group

Learn more here: https://bit.ly/realitytvonlinecourse

To catch a glimpse inside the course and to offer my final thanks for your time and energy spent inside this book journey, I've got one more gift for you!

Enjoy this exclusive full interview with America's Got Talent Season 2 Runner Up, Cas Haley and hear more about his experience, as well as, his top tips and advice for hopeful contestants. To watch the full video, scan the QR code below or visit: https://scnv.io/cashaley

ACKNOWLEDGEMENTS

Thank you

I'm grateful to so many who offered their time and energy to this project and want to personally thank a few talented contributors.

Thank you to Cas Haley, Tippy Balady, Katrina Cain, Griffin Holtby, Jo James, Jessica Manalo, Tori Martin and Matt New for your openness in sharing your past reality singing show experience. Your kindness and willingness to support others on their journey is greatly appreciated.

Thank you to my friends and expert industry colleagues, Meagan D'Von Funk, Megan Kuhar, Adam Pickrell, Jonathon Ragsdale, Tiffany VanBoxtel and Katie Zaccardi for your generosity in sharing your expertise inside this book. Thank you also to Cheryl B. Engelhardt for lighting a fire under me to take this idea to completion and Angela Mastrogiacomo for reminding me how "lit up" I get when I talk about performance!

Thank you to the many who supported my book efforts, including Caroline Laughlin, Kate McKay, Tyler Lajoie, Jen at Wild Words Formatting and my Launch Team who committed their time to help me share this book with the world.

Thank you also to my SPS Family, Chandler Bolt and my rockstar coaches Lisa Zelenak and Sean Sumner. You've challenged me to evolve in fresh ways that have forever changed my life.

Last but certainly not least, I thank my family for your patience and support, through the often long days when I was "in the zone" to get this passion project complete. I'm sincerely grateful for your belief in me and love you with all my heart.

ABOUT THE AUTHOR

Brianna Ruelas is a Dallas Based Strategy Consultant for Performing Artists & Reality TV Music Coach, Singer-Songwriter, Author & Online Course Creator. She and her husband also own Victor Hugo's Restaurant and Bar in Dallas.

As a singer and performer for thirty years, Brianna has studied internationally and performed all genres, from jazz to rock to pop, received a BA in Theatre Arts from Pepperdine University, and spent years honing her musical theatre chops. After graduating college, Brianna departed from the theatre to pursue music as a solo artist and also worked as a commercial voiceover actor. Brianna has fronted her own rock band and experienced the reality television craze in its early days, as a Top 100 finalist on American Idol, Season 4.

Brianna's expertise and background as a Singer/Songwriter, Vocal & Performance Coach and Restaurant Owner, led her to mentor and consult indie artists, to equip them with online business strategies for sustainable music careers. She is passionate about encouraging others on their music journey and igniting them towards creating personal and professional success.

Learn more at https://www.briannaruelasmusic.com/ and follow her on Instagram or Facebook @briannaruelasmusic

Made in the USA
Columbia, SC
29 October 2020

23670027R00098